# Twenty-first Century Learning by Doing

# Twenty-first Century Learning by Doing

*By*
**Judith M. Meloy**
*Castleton State College, Vermont, USA*

SENSE PUBLISHERS
ROTTERDAM/BOSTON/TAIPEI

A C.I.P. record for this book is available from the Library of Congress.

ISBN: 978-94-6209-096-5 (paperback)
ISBN: 978-94-6209-097-2 (hardback)
ISBN: 978-94-6209-098-9 (e-book)

Published by: Sense Publishers,
P.O. Box 21858,
3001 AW Rotterdam,
The Netherlands
https://www.sensepublishers.com/

*Printed on acid-free paper*

I read your book on the qualitative dissertation during my coursework and found it to be very useful.

**Dennis** McCunney, graduate student, Morgan State University

JUDITH M. MELOY

# TWENTY-FIRST CENTURY LEARNING BY DOING

The most important thing I learned from my research experience is that nothing is more precious, valuable, and meaningful than my research participants. Nothing can surpass humanity. I always think it is a privilege to be able to interview someone or observe someone and finally report what I see and hear in that person. I believe there is an unspoken trust between the participant and the researcher. It is the researcher's responsibility to maintain the trust. In my opinion, the only way to maintain the trust is to present the authentic image of the participant. I need to be true to my participants. I have to be true to the data – what my participants communicated with me. To a great extent, their words were guiding my thinking and writing, leading the direction of my research.

**Wanju** Huang

Best wishes to you in researching and writing this book. I, as your other correspondents I presume, recently finished my qualitative dissertation and found the adventure to be combinations of clarity and confusion, immersion and detachment, excitement and frustration. In the end, though, I believe I found my voice and was able to portray the findings through a depth of understanding that only the qualitative approach lends itself to.

**Victor** Fisher

1.   Am I the type of person who can deductively figure out "who did it" half way through a movie, or do I figure it out at the end after hearing all the characters' stories and the plot has thickened to the boiling point?

2.   If I were investigating a crime scene, would I ask each witness the same questions in the same order or would I let a witness' response dictate what the next question would be?

3.   Do I like adding the numbers, or do I like how the numbers add up?

**Cassandra** Quigley

You will have moments of panic when you wonder "What does all this mean? Why is it important? Who really cares about all this?" Doubts about your work

vii

are actually pretty healthy! I would have never thought that. Why? Because doubt forces you to reconsider, to ponder your interpretations, to reflect on your analysis and comments from members of your committee…no matter how obscure. Taking a step back is necessary at all stages of the process.

**Isabelle** Drewelow

# PREFACE

What this book is *not:*

- a mixed methods study
- a 'right answers' manual
- only for graduate students
- only for professors working with graduate students
- a straightforward read
- an "academic text"
- like any other book on qualitative research

This book *is*:

- the result of a general query, the focus of which was the experience of undertaking qualitative research for one's doctorate
- the result of getting acquainted – through words, nuance, and email – with the thinking, feeling, and experiencing of 69 correspondents from 25 states, Puerto Rico and Canada

This book offers:

- stories of "quants" going "qual"
- stories of quals going creative
- reflections about data collection and analysis
- perceptions of "insiders" and "outsiders"
- perspectives of learning by doing from mathematicians, musicians, and ESL colleagues
- perspectives of learning from those who were also first generation college students, administrators, and teachers
- descriptions, for example, of course assignments, committees, IRB boards, technology, advisors and participants, as well as "justification" and "self-as-learner"
- descriptions of ongoing thinking and decision making
- descriptions – detailed, candid, and courageous – of the emotional "roller coaster" and personal changes the process of learning by doing reveals

In short, this volume contains in only lightly edited form the thoughts of individual human beings who grappled with or who are completing their lives as the "human instrument" in an attempt to make contributions beyond themselves, so to honor the work, their participants, and our human potential.

**Jessica:** While I learned many lessons throughout the dissertation process, the most important for me was the way in which my relationship with the participants unfolded and ultimately shaped the very interpretation of the data.

# TABLE OF CONTENTS: GENERAL

# TABLE OF CONTENTS: SPECIFIC TO INTRODUCTION

# ACKNOWLEDGEMENTS

To Michel Lokhorst, Desha Lourens, and all at SENSE Publishing: the correspondents and I thank you deeply and sincerely for welcoming us and expediting our support for thinking, learning and doing. To the many individuals who inquired about becoming a part of this book, and to the many professors/advisors/researchers and mentors of novice qualitative researchers around the world, I cannot thank you enough for your interest in supporting others. To the 69 individuals, "my" correspondents, who continued to pour so much of their intelligence, insight, passion and humanity into their letters, you know there is no book without you. Finally, to Naomi Silverman: you remain my hero.

# INTRODUCTION

The environment for and experiencing of learning about qualitative research has changed immensely during the past twenty-five years. No longer is it the case that a few students in a few universities are struggling to find some professor, somewhere, to help them. No longer is it the case that what doesn't make sense and what isn't working are the only things students learning about qualitative research have to say. What is the case, and what I will briefly describe to you in the next few pages, are the especial qualities of twenty-first century learning by doing. More than three hundred individuals answered the query to help me complete this work; sixty-nine committed to the task. Because I received an abundance of insight, description, and "advice", you will note that the correspondents' work appears from the very beginning, leading the text by focusing your attention on its themes. The correspondents' words and experience, concerns and emphases "grew" the text that is before you, shaping this one example of the possible representation of my "findings". (The detailed thinking and analysis leading to its ultimate form is further described in Appendix I.).

With this introduction, then, I offer a brief history of our project. I will also tell you that what you read, as well as how you choose to read it has been made available and organized with the correspondents' direct as well as implicit help. For example, given that the thinking and reflection shared in the sixty-nine letters comprising my data set offered ideas heavily contextual and connected to thoughts "belonging in more than one place," I was unable to construct a thoroughly linear text, i.e., "here's the scoop, from A–Z." I was, however, able to incorporate the correspondents' thinking across all sections of this book because they reflected on so many aspects of the experience of learning by doing. So, even while you are reading this introduction, which you might assume would be "all mine", you will become aware of the variety of data analyses and attempts to organize and portray the correspondents' thinking in ways that honor what they shared with me while supporting your ability to find, apprehend, think with, and use it. From all of us, then, this book is for you, for *your* purposes, whether you be an undergraduate learning basic principles for the first time or a doctoral student with previous research experiences. This book will make more sense, however, if I begin by telling you about ours.

WHY THIS BOOK?

The answer to this question resides in my long-term interest in sharing *"how it **feels** and what it **means** to do qualitative research for the doctoral dissertation" (Meloy, 1994; 2002).* However, the letters of 21st century correspondents provided much evidence that specific support for *understanding* is no longer issue; these correspondents are focused on thinking and doing. There are many reasons why this is so. Firstly, there are many departments, schools, colleges, and universities supporting individuals who are teaching, doing, and learning qualitative research from the undergraduate through the doctoral levels. Additionally, many of these 21st century correspondents have had experience with qualitative research (QR) *prior* to their doctoral work, while those new to QR in their doctoral programs report a variety of opportunities they either took advantage of or created for themselves in order to gain enough background knowledge and experience to do it well, e.g., working as research assistants, completing interesting assignments in their course work, and conducting mini-projects, pilot and independent studies. The researchers you meet in this book write about finding one's voice, wanting to make contributions to one's field, and recognizing the effects and benefits of doing QR for their thesis far beyond the completion of the degree. They talk analysis, reflect on the role of self and theory, and participate(d) in insider-outsider research; more than several seriously enjoy methodology for its own sake. Qualitative research has "arrived"; guidance and support for the process, once direly sought, is now common. A book describing what is now common, however, is not.

I know you will be impressed with the willingness, ability, and candor of the correspondents who have made themselves available, and hence vulnerable, to you. I am honored to be introducing them – and their mentors, families, friends, and participants – as your guide. I am proud of their thinking, feeling, and writing; I am humbled by their trust in our endeavor.

**Jim B:** I was very fortunate to have a strong support network of family and friends during the dissertation writing process. I had one classmate in many of the same courses. When it came time for comprehensive qualifying exams and dissertation writing, we set up several meetings a week to get together at a coffee shop or the library to work on our writing. The accountability of having a study partner who was expecting me to meet at a certain time and place was very helpful. It was also a significant support to have family members who understood the dissertation writing process. My wife (Carin Barber – also a respondent for your book) was authoring her dissertation at the same time; we spent many nights closing down the local coffee shop writing in the evenings after work.

HISTORY

It was in early December, 2010 when I received several emails asking if I was ever going to write another book. Knowing my spring schedule was light, I chose to commence 2011 determined both to get my "author's query" published in the *Chronicle of Higher Education* and conclude the research necessary to complete a book. Within a day of finishing the former I did receive a few responses from the posting on a research blog to which the *Chronicle* had directed me. Although I had decided not immediately to go to the American Educational Research Association (AERA) divisions and special interest groups (SIGS), always hoping to locate individuals both within and outside the field of education, by the second week in January response remained so thin that I moved forward, contacting the AREA division vice presidents. More than several responded immediately, sharing the query with their list serves. No doubt Professor William A Firestone of the Rutgers Graduate School of Education will recognize more than several names on the correspondent list, as I was immediately inundated – and happily so – with what must have been almost every new member in Division L.

Even though interest was high, commitments to participate did not arrive as quickly. By the end of January, I contacted the Qualitative Research SIG of AERA (of which I was a former chair). Deb Ceglowski forwarded the query to our listserv. Then, of course, the commitments from the first two groups started coming in. I found myself in the unfortunate but grateful position of having to stop accepting potential correspondents within the week; two exceptions squeezed in under the wire. I asked everyone to send their letters no later than the end of March.

Between March 15th – 31st, give or take 48 hours, all letters were in. I had been making my lists and checking them twice. I had numbers and names and no ABC order. I made a copy of each letter and put it aside, because I wanted to be able to return to the "whole" as I received it with no codes or color schemes forcing my attention to certain aspects of the material. I hole-punched the original letters and put them in two large, three ring notebooks, separating each with a piece of colored paper. On April 1, 2011 I sat down on the couch to read. (The thinking, analyses, and interactions that led to the final appearance of this book are further described in Appendix I.)


THEMES

### *The Overarching Theme*

In almost every letter, the correspondents discuss, describe, or reflect upon their decision making, whether it be in their very first research course or after their thesis defense. Sometimes their choices were clear or "obvious" to them; sometimes, they were a source of ambiguity and stress; often, true insight was the result of "hindsight." I would suggest if you do not like to make decisions, if you want a clear cut path, then QR is not the way to go. On the other hand, this book is full of rich, supportive examples that will surely bolster anyone's confidence in his/her ability to continue.


### *Questions as Explicit and Subtle Themes*

Because the correspondents' letters did so much more than address the 7 focus questions (see page 5), which were only meant to stimulate their thinking, you will find a myriad of additional themes across their writing (see subject index). Using Jessica's abbreviated letter (see Appendix I) as an example of the writing I received, you will also notice that numerous ideas can be found within one portion of a letter, e.g., Jessica discussed the use of technology in the response to the question about support (Appendix I, p. 149). Topical headings, therefore, are only general signifiers of content that answers additional questions such as:

- Does identifying with a group mean you can better understand them? Yourself?
- "What is a quant like you doing in a place like this?"
- What if English is *not* your native language?
- How can a course assignment change your life?
- How did you handle exposure to illegal activity?
- How did you come to select your topic?
- Describe your experience collecting data in a foreign country?
- What kinds of decisions did you have to negotiate with your professor/advisor?
- Coding, coding, coding!
- What did you learn "in the end" or "in hindsight"?
- What do Atlas and NVivo mean to a qualitative dissertator?
- What is your personal story? What can we learn from it?
- Being a strong writer is not enough, is it?
- How did you make sense of what didn't make sense?
- Explain how you constructed a new method/theory/framework?
And finally,
- What *are* the issues with chapter 4/data analysis?

*Summary*

In this book I am trusting that even the novice researcher has "come a long way". My job is to help you, the reader, follow the details of topic and threads of humanity across issues confronting the correspondents as they describe learning by doing. My job is to make their experiences accessible to you in a number of ways, so that you can enter the text through the tables of content or indices, through the correspondents themselves or the issues, through brief excerpts or rich descriptions. This is a book designed for you to read *your* way, to access *your* way, to *enjoy* your way. It is *not* a book to be read in one sitting or begun on page one and read through its entirety; you probably will not want to as there are so many words on the page and so many voices asking to heard. Notice who is speaking. Listen. Pause often. Think. Take genuine care of your learning self and the humanity of your 69 new colleagues; please respect their candor and sincerity. I guarantee as you get to know them, one or two will become close companions if not good friends to you. The material here is that rich; these individuals are that thoughtful.

AUDIENCES

This book is for anyone who has an interest in the intellectual and emotional work learning and doing QR is – that means students as well as faculty members, parents as well as friends, and even, perhaps, our participants. I paraphrase **Sheila,** who wrote that "what appears so cleanly and neatly on the page" is *not* a reflection of its creation, i.e., the midnight hours, the rewrites, the "struggle to get it right". *TWENTY-FIRST CENTURY LEARNING BY DOING* is one attempt to do just that. My work was not to define my correspondents' offerings, but rather to make their thinking and doing accessible to you. For the correspondents, their work is largely done; we leave the rest up to you, your colleagues and professors. There is much good stuff here to think with and use, i.e., much is transferable, but that "what" is up to you, as it should be. All flaws in presentation and omission are mine alone.

## STRUCTURE

### *The Original Questions*

The final structure of this book comes from a merging of seven focus questions, below, with the attention the correspondents gave to them as well as the additional issues they wanted to bring to your attention. Although the correspondents were given much encouragement to "tell me anything you would like to" about the experience of doing QR, many responded either loosely or specifically to the following questions.

1. How did you learn about qualitative research?
2. Why did you choose it?
3. What issues/obstacles/choices did you face once you made your decision to use it?
4. What supports for it exist at your university – Alumni? Qualitative research faculty? Conferences? Internet connections?
5. What methodological questions were raised by your work? How did you answer them?
6. What does the final form of your dissertation look like? Traditional? Collaborative? "Novel"? Was it your choice or your committee's?
7. Are there any stories *you'd* like to share from which others might learn?

### *Framework*

Because it is easier to think in a complex way than it is to write and simultaneously be coherent in a complex way, I decided to use these questions to help me build the overall structure of the book, although not necessarily in a singular or sequential fashion.

- Section One is divided into three parts, responding to questions one, two and six, respectively, i.e., when the correspondents learned about QR, why they chose QR, and what their dissertations look like. In each part, I provide two means of accessing the responses, "quantitative" and "qualitative", depending upon your needs and interests. Each highlights a different analytical "cut" at the data and showcases several obvious methodological strengths and challenges for your consideration and discussion.
- Section Two is also divided into three parts, each of which contains descriptions of some of the issues and obstacles one faces in the process of learning by doing.

- Section Three responds to the fourth question about supports for QR.
- Section Four targets question five, methodological issues.
- Section Five emerges from the correspondents' writing and is about writing.
- Section Six presents a variety of responses to question seven.
- There are three appendices and two detailed indices, by correspondent and subject.
- References

## STYLE

In order to best understand how I have composed this book, I ask that you attend to **three major stylistic changes that purposefully do *not* conform to the style guidelines of the American Psychological Association (APA).**

### *Abbreviations*

The first change is the frequent use of abbreviations for terms that are continuously used across all letters. In order to keep this book affordable, I hoped that using abbreviations would eliminate a few pages and not distract the reader too much.

### *Figure 1*

Abbreviations used in the Book

| QD | = | qualitative dissertation | qual | = | qualitative |
|----|---|--------------------------|-------|---|-------------|
| QM | = | qualitative method/ology/s/ies | quant | = | quantitative |
| QR | = | qualitative research | LR | = | lit review |
| QS | = | qualitative study/ies | QI | = | qual inquiry |

### *Contractions*

The second change is to leave in many of the contractions the correspondents used in their letter writing: wasn't, didn't, couldn't, that's, etc. Their writing was an informal letter to me through which they are talking to you, the reader, as if you were right there with them. There is nothing academic or formal in this goal or that writing style (Lyons, 1984). I want the correspondents to remain "user-friendly;" I need to use their language as they shared it with me. Contractions diminish neither their intelligence nor insight.

### *Third to First Person "Glide"*

The third change emerged while I was writing. I found I was eliminating quotation marks as well as virtually all assertions that were placing me between the correspondents' thinking and your apprehension of it. The result of this "disappearance" became what I call a 3rd to 1st person "glide". Examples 1 and 2 below display my decision making as it would be applied to the type of "interference"

I am describing. Please note that the correspondent's name is bold; my voice is italicized. Readers will find this format on rare occasions in this book.

1. *Across the 69 correspondents completing letters for this book, several described their learning as* **Mary** *does*: My program required three introductory research courses, which I loved!
2. **Tom** *writes*: We had research classes in …; I found it difficult…

In this book, the statements look and read as follows:

1. **Mary**'s program required three introductory research courses, which I loved!
2. **Tom** had research classes in….; I found it difficult…

The correspondent's name in **bold** signifies the individual is the author of the passage you are reading/ thinking with. Examples 3 and 4 below depict again how I have minimized the "interference" by eliminating any introductory material. *Your job is to make the following mind shift: 'When I see a name in* **bold** *I am to think "I/ my/we/our". '* There are no quotation marks because the entire sentence(s) is directly from the correspondent him/herself.

1. **Debra**'s doctoral program required that I complete four methodology courses.
2. (read as: "Debra = MY doctoral program …required that I…".).
3. **Donna** always felt as though I had enormous support.
4. (read as: "Donna = I always felt I…").

I do realize what I am asking, i.e., when you see a name, you learn the author of the passage while you are simultaneously reading his/her voice. You need to "glide into" that correspondent's mind for sensemaking to occur. I believe this move gets you closer to the minds and hearts of the correspondents.

- Notice that *any italicized portion* is me introducing or connecting text; it won't happen often! Sometimes, you will also see a box around my words to further break up the lemming-like progression of words.
- Notice the correspondents' names are **bold**, making them easier to locate!
- Notice I have eliminated quotation marks around direct quotations because the correspondents have done the vast majority of writing in this book! I believe that quotation marks in this case would make their thinking an "artifact" in need of mediation and explication *when the singular purpose of this research and book is to make their voices as accessible and living as possible; their words and thinking ought to flow into you as if you were reading their letters, as if you were their first audience.* I have done my best to ensure that you are.

Try practicing the 3rd to 1st glide with one more example!

**Jim B**'s thesis format is fairly traditional, although I divided the findings into two chapters for better organization. **Mary** hopes my traditional dissertation has the feel of a story. The format was a committee decision/requirement. *This last statement is also true for* **Sandy**, but I did have plenty of freedom in writing up the findings and discussion sections.

I hope I have conveyed some of the excitement I feel no longer transporting the correspondents' letters to "my" pages but rather flowing their thinking for our mutual purpose directly toward you. To start us off "whole-ly" then, to show you why their uninterrupted and unmediated thinking is so important to this book, I offer one of the original letters as I received it, title and all; it serves as an individual and contextual introduction to the entirety of the QR experience and the book ahead.

## LETTER FROM AN ANGLO RESEARCHER – BY LISA HEUVEL

Anyone who has lived and breathed the dissertation process knows it is in a class by itself – no pun intended. Doctoral study and dissertation writing form a singular initiation process into the mysteries of academe; much like weddings, breakups, or pregnancies, survivors have experiences to share. My message is for dissertation-bound students contemplating research studies across cultures, particularly when these studies impact relationships with friends and colleagues.

My dissertation was a phenomenological study of the worldviews, experiences, and teaching methodologies of faculty members in an innovative seminar for K-12 teachers. This program presented Virginia Indian history and cultures encompassing the pre-colonial era to the present from a Native perspective. I interviewed most of the American Indian and Anglo faculty members who participated in the initial 2007 and 2008 seminars held on university campuses. This multi-generational group of tribal and academic experts focused on replacing myth and cultural stereotypes in classrooms with accurate information about Virginia Indians, their history and cultures.

It took years of collaborating with Native colleagues on other projects to develop the necessary trust relationships for this research, partly because of the lasting effects of colonialism and 20th century segregation in Virginia Indian communities statewide. Strong feelings of advocacy had motivated me to apply to a doctoral program in higher education administration in order to partner more effectively in education for, about, and with Virginia Indians. After the prerequisite research courses, I decided that qualitative research was the best way to explore my research questions about their teaching methodologies with the study participants. These educators all had worked with me previously, and I gained advance permission from tribal leaders to move forward. It all looked good on paper; I would conduct my interviews using carefully vetted questions, remembering to uphold my protocol and responsibilities as a researcher.

I was familiar with Virginia Indian history through oral as well as written historical accounts, and felt as prepared as possible acknowledge my preconceptions. In retrospect, I began conceptualizing my research questions, conceptual framework, and methods unaware of the full complexity of historical trauma and unresolved grief, stereotypes, and racism participants were about to share in coming months. However, more complex aspects of social research soon emerged in relation to these culturally sensitive issues. I did not know what lay ahead in working with my own deep-seated feelings regarding social justice, and in taking qualitative research theory into application with people I respected. Here's a summary of what I learned though this experience.

If I were in front of a class of doctoral students beginning such projects, I'd start with two words: Assume nothing. Remember that injunction each step of the way. Think through in a detailed way what research protocol will best protect your integrity as a researcher and protect your participants, and consider it from their vantage point. For many of them as for you, this will be a first-time experience. Initially, participants may not understand the long-term significance of their collaboration. Whether they know you well or not, they may trust you to the point of not asking about such outcomes and their ramifications. If they choose anonymity, what steps will you take to protect them as fully as possible? If they wish to be identified publicly, it means their names and information will be forever tied to your dissertation, your findings, and your professional path. This is even more reason to be rigorous.

Hammer all this out with your chair and your committee. We talk about saturation in collecting data and analyzing it, but I advocate saturation in startup, using the following strategies. Read extensively about cross-cultural qualitative and action research in other social sciences, especially anthropology, because it will enable you to see more options and outcomes. Make sure you can explain your intentions accurately and clearly before you go to your first interview. If you are working with people you know, the protocol is even more important: Friendships and collegial relationships are at stake. Do not allow those bonds to relax your vigilance. Instead, help your study participants to understand why it is vital for you to follow guidelines.

If you are working in another community with different norms and values than your own culture, you face additional hurdles that should not be underestimated, particularly if you are inexperienced in ethnographic studies and oral history. Talk frankly with your chair. If there are differences in how your coursework and your chair address audit trails and "researcher as instrument" statements, <u>then</u> discuss those differences. Then you know up front what to do as you tackle whatever personal cognitive or emotional dissonance arises from your research as you hear and process your participants' words. You may have emotions that surface along the way from your own worldview and background. You may internalize stories about prejudice and injustice in others' experiences. However, feeling ambivalent about your role as an academic researcher is counter-productive. It is far better to model and explain how participants' rights can be effectively protected through proper protocols. Be vigilant in member checking during and following all interviews. In terms of data, remember that your initial findings are subject to change and stay open to that possibility. Keep a journal throughout the development of your research process. As you generate data and analyze it, write memos. You can document your thoughts and emotions in relation to your findings.

Remember that if you don't voice concerns or confusion about culturally based issues – or any issues – as they arise, your chair and committee members cannot guide you through them. Moreover, other doctoral students may operate under different criteria and expectations. Don't assume that anyone else's research path matches yours.

Last but far from least, keep your participants informed as you reach milestones such as dissertation submission and defense. It is crucial to honor your participants and their voices throughout the process, and to guarantee their access to your work. Sincerely, Lisa

## CONCLUSION

**Lisa**'s letter is a 21st century "table of contents". It is a story of a competent learner who was confident she had done what she needed to do in order to put herself intelligently in the field on an issue important to her. Being a 21st century "human instrument" however, has only gotten more complex with her – and our – choices of topics, settings, and participants. By beginning with her own experience and concluding with attention to her participants, Lisa demonstrates that which so many in the following pages will share with you: if and when you do this work, you will change. What, and who you attend to will change, significantly, and probably more than once. In a learning experience where so much is uncertain, change is guaranteed. Whether "different", "transformed", or "more of a scholar/professional", you will change.

Our purpose with this book is to accompany you while *you* change, to shine a light where you might need it, to be a friend when there is no one there who "gets it", to provide that insight, which keeps eluding you. We will be here when the nagging doubts you have – about your capacity (am I too young, too old, first-generation, male, female, quant, 'outsider', 'insider') or your decision making (can I create something new, how do I justify my choice among these methods, how can I best protect my participants) – leave you believing the decision you made to undertake qualitative research was the wrong one. More than 300 individuals initially responded to the call to support you. Eighteen graduate students and 51 Ph.Ds. and Ed.Ds. committed to the task in April of 2011. I am thrilled to introduce them briefly to you across the next few pages. Before I do, however, I want you to know that in the pages beyond their "facts" you will be privy to candid descriptions of much complexity, some naiveté, as well as sincere insight gleaned from the integrated processes of doing-questioning-thinking-deciding-doing again that comprise the work of qualitative research, the work of learning by doing; please respect their efforts. I know their experiences will encourage you to proceed with your researches and provide you the wisdom to do so well. No doubt you will let us know if we have succeeded.

Sincerely,
Judy Meloy
judy.meloy@castleton.edu

## INTRODUCTION TO THE CORRESPONDENTS

*(Note: Dissertations listed below are unpublished unless otherwise noted)*

* = AERA Distinguished Dissertation Award recipient

***Crystal** Laura's "subject" is her brother and how a middle class black family dealt with his wanting to drop out of high school.
*"Bad Boy": My baby brother and the social ecology of "difference"* (2011: University of Illinois)

**Jim O**live (James) interviewed "marginalized" individuals, wondering where the best place to do so would be.
*Life histories of gay, lesbian, bisexual, and queer postsecondary students who choose to persist: Education against the tide.* (2009: University of Dayton)

**Sarah** Deaver provides the only photograph, a page from her visual journal.
*Reflective visual journaling during art therapy and counseling internships.* (2009: Old Dominion University)

**Ronn**ald Hallett is "a quant"; he was "surprised" at the fit/ability of QR to make a difference.
*Educating transient youth: Influence of residential instability on educational resilience.* (2009: University of Southern California)

**Carin** Barber is a student affairs administrator who wrote about getting practice with interviewing.
*Culture, surprise, and adaptation: Examining undergraduate students' matriculation processes.* (2010: Eastern Michigan University)

**Nancy** Gray provides rich description of how she "came to love" QR; she also writes about the "self as instrument" section in her thesis.
*The role of school leaders in teacher-peer social relationships: A critical collective case study.* (2009: University of Idaho)

**Karen R**oss, a grad student at Indiana University, is keenly interested in methodology as subject.

**Tom** (Thomas) Conway, a former social studies teacher, claims an "outsider" role in his research.
*The electrical and technology curriculum of an urban charter high school and its impact for the female in academic and trade settings.* (2010: Saint Joseph's University)

**Veronica** Richard's experience can be summed up in the word "relationships".
*Using (re)valuing methodology to understand content area literacy immersion (CALI): A journey with preservice secondary content area teachers.* (2010: University of Northern Colorado)

**Ginny** (Virginia) Cottrill, an "experienced writer" and grad student at Ohio University, writes about…writing!

**Liz** (Elizabeth) Farley-Ripple, an experienced quantitative researcher, explains the qual-quant connection and the impact of her choices from the very beginning through to her future.
*Accountability, evidence, and school district decision-making.* (2008: University of Pennsylvania)

**Roxanne** Hughes' table of contents can be found in Appendix II.
*The process of choosing science, technology, engineering, and mathematics careers by undergraduate women: A narrative life history analysis.* (2010: Florida State University)

**Alex** Medler, whose project was large – "and largely quantitative" – shares his detailed thinking about coding.
*A strategic coalitions frame: Conflict over education policy within and between coalitions.* (2008: University of Colorado, Boulder)

**Francesca** Durand responds specifically to the focus questions.
*P-16 initiatives: A policy discourse analysis approach to state level education reform.* (2011: SUNY Albany)

**Julie** Levine, a math teacher and current grad student at the George Washington University, also replies to the focus questions.

**Kandace** Knudson's contribution focuses on how we choose to title our work.
*Community college freshman composition instructors' choices of readings: The importance of context.* (2005: University of California, Davis)

**Grover** McDaniel writes that he listened to his advisor; the rest, as they say, is history!
*Emotions and the military training instructor: A view from the inside.* (2009: Capella University)

**Cindy** (Cynthia) Epperson discusses the challenges of her decision to complete multiple case studies and collect data in Viet Nam.
*An analysis of the community college concept in the Socialist Republic of Viet Nam.* (2010: University of Missouri – St. Louis)

**Donna** Sayman's research grew out of a conversation with her son about stereotypes.
*Man enough to care: Experiences of men working in the female dominated profession of nursing in the state of Oklahoma.* (2009: Oklahoma State University)

**Angela** Frusciante, a first generation college student, describes her experience with QR as the "journey of finding my own voice" while appreciating the "location of the responsibility" in QR as being in herself, the human instrument and decision maker.
*An analytic case study of the evaluation reports of a comprehensive community initiative.* (2004: University of Maryland, College Park)

**Lisa** Weaver does not find what she thought she would in her research.
*How communication and sensemaking in an academic community of practice affects individuals' professional identities.* (2006: Penn State)

**Sandy** (Sandra) Blanchette completed a master's thesis using QM, building expertise for the completion of her QD.
*Space and power in the ivory tower: Decision making in public higher education.* (2010: University of Massachusetts Boston)

**Richard** Grogan researched independent service station operators; he shares many thoughts about the work along the way.
*On the road to sustainability: From vision to action in the sustainability transition.* (2010: Michigan State University)

**Amy** Orange has taught an introduction to QR class; gaining entry and protecting participants were challenges for her.
*Program improvement in NCLB: A case study of transformation of policy intentions.* (2011: University of Virginia)

**Debra** Ackerman writes about "the things I learned by doing", succinctly summing up the purpose of this book. Through her letter, I thought: "every QR study has a 'back story'", whether it is explicit or not.

*"The learning never stops": Lessons from military child development centers for teacher professional development.* (2006: Rutgers University)

**Xyan**athe Neider completed a QD in part "to heal my own diseased thinking" related to stereotypes of Middle Eastern students on a college campus.

*"When you come here, it is still like it is their space: Exploring the experiences of students of Middle Eastern heritages in post-9/11 US higher education.* (2010: Washington State University)*

**Kj** (Kelley-Jean Strong-) Rhoads, among other contributions, describes her coding process.

*Transformational classroom leadership: Adding a new piece of fabric to the educational leadership quilt.* (2011: California State University, Sacramento)

**Corey** (James C) McKenna worked hard to keep his dissertation under 500 pages!

*The development and implementation of an integrated curriculum at an elementary math, science, and technology magnet school.* (2007: University of California, Santa Barbara)

*Yeon Sun (**Ellie**) Ro worked hard to keep her longitudinal ethnographic dissertation under 600 pages; she also appreciated collaboration during analysis.

*Navigating a bilingual/biliterate childhood: A longitudinal study of three second-generation young learners in the U.S.* (2010: University of Illinois, Urbana-Champaign)

**Annie** Jonas shares about how so much of the QR experience seems to be "one step forward, two steps back"; she does not think that is a bad thing.

*Practices of two experiential teachers in secondary schools in an era of accountability.* (2011: Western Carolina University)

**Sheila** Fram wanted an interdisciplinary degree and made it happen.

*"Look, it takes practices": The socialization of graduate students.* (2008: Arizona State University)

**Cassie** Quigley offers context to highlight context as the point of her outsider/insider study.

*In their words: An exploration into how the construction of congruent Third Space creates an environment for employment of scientific discourse in urban, African-American kindergarten girls.* (2010: Indiana University)

**Jessie** Guidry Baginski answered my questions, lauding her "great, caring faculty".

*The Hurricane Katrina volunteer experience: Inclusion into life narratives of young adults.* (2011: Cleveland State University). Published in the Ohio Electronic Thesis Database.

**Vic**tor Fisher chose QR because he wanted to learn what he did not already know.

*School improvement from the central office: A view of the five year strategic planning process in selected West Virginia counties.* (2010: West Virginia University)

**Jodi** Fisler shares specific advice, having just completed her "non-positivisitic" QR dissertation.

*The elephant in the room: Deconstructing the place of conservatives in the student affairs profession.* (2011: The College of William and Mary)

**Madeline** Ortiz-Rodriguez wrote three letters, discussing the overall experience, data analysis, and perseverance.

*In search of a mathematics discourse model: Constructing mathematics knowledge through online discussion forums.* (2008: University of Florida) PROQUEST 3347164

**Shaunna** Payne Gold found QR to be life changing; she offers four "priorities" to consider while doing.

*The spiritual development of nonheterosexual undergraduate students.* (2010: The George Washington University)

**Isabelle** Drewelow used IM to collect her data!

*The influence of instructed learning on American college students' cultural assumptions about the French language and people.* (2009: University of Wisconsin-Madison)

**Jessica** Lester recently defended, acknowledging she is "a part of the methodological choices I make".

*The discursive construction of autism: Contingent meanings of autism and therapeutic talk.* (2011: University of Tennessee)

**Michelle** McConkey, a grad student at the beginning of this work, has successfully defended her dissertation.

*An examination of the emotional competency and emotional practices of four elementary general music teachers.* (2012: Arizona State University)

**Monica Jean** Alaniz asserts that QR is "necessary to get to the heart of the matter."

*From out of the Field: Migrant student success in a post-secondary community college setting.* (2010: University of Texas, San Antonio) Available at ProQuest (UMI No. 3433201)

**Aaron** Coe relates a conversation with his advisor prior to his thesis defense.

*Pedagogy of scholarship in higher education administration.* (2011: Arizona State University) Available in ProQuest.

**ANON**ymous: refers to any one of the correspondents at any time, *my* choice.

**Amanda** Corbin-Staton utilizes meta-interpretation for her doctoral dissertation.

*Contexts of parental involvement: An interpretive synthesis of qualitative literature using the meta-interpretation method.* (2009: The George Washington University) http://www.gradworks.umi.com/33/44/3344879.html

**Megan** Ohler, a colleague in Vermont, details her experience getting IRB approval.

*One too many: College students share their experiences of being deemed intoxicated beyond control.* (2009: University of Vermont)

**Rosaire** Ifedi pondered her thesis topic until she mentioned an idea to several colleagues and friends who simply "gushed" that she should do it. So she did!

*African-born women faculty in the United States: Lives in contradiction.* (2007: Ashland University)

**Anabella** Martinez, among her answers, writes about a qualitative researcher's "basic instinct".

*Learning through research: How a summer undergraduate research experience informs undergraduate students' views of research and learning.* (2009: Teachers College, Columbia)

**Kristan** Venegas, a first generation college student, finds her learning further inspired by text and film.

*Aid and admission: Financial aid narratives of eight pre-college urban Latinas.* (2005: University of Southern California, Los Angeles.)

**Cassandra** Crute completed a self-directed mini study of a church-related experience, "getting happy", in order to develop her research skills.

*Leading entrepreneurially: Understanding how community college leaders identify with and related to entrepreneurial leadership.* (2010: Mercer University)

**Isabeau** Iqbal, a grad student at the University of British Columbia, addresses technology.

**Angela LV** (Angela M. Lopez-Velasquez) writes in detail and at length, serving as a role model for ESL colleagues.

*The reading development and comprehension of English and Spanish text among four Hispanic bilingual first-graders.* (2008: University of Illinois, Urbana-Champaign)

**Katherine** Mansfield, "told" she could only study "people like herself" lets us know she chose to listen to herself, instead.

*Troubling social justice in a single-sex public school: An ethnography of an emerging school culture.* (2011: The University of Texas, Austin)

**Hilary** Levey Friedman describes what must be the epitome of "prolonged engagement" and "immersion with the data".

*Playing to win: Raising children in a competitive culture.* (2009: Princeton University)

**Tiffany** (Leger-Rodriguez) found doing QR "HARD!", but satisfying, because "most studies in special education are quantitative!"

*Paraprofessional preparation and supervision in special education.* (2010: University of California, Riverdale)

**Joan** Q. Minnis wanted her dissertation "to be a reflection of my 'lived experiences'".

*Ethical and moral decision making: Praxis and hermeneutics for school leaders.* (2011: University of South Florida)

**Keith** Higa muses over "good" data and shares some thoughts about program completion.

*What art compels: Students' artistic experiences in an alternative school.* (2011: Oklahoma State University)

**Michele** Paynter Paise's experience reminds us all that 'life happens while we are making other plans.'

*Six beginning music teachers' music teacher role identities.* (2010: Arizona State University)

**Kristen** Chorba, a graduate student, shares her thoughts about writing.

**Monica** Morita offers specific advice related to those who engage with student athletes.

*A study of Pacific Islander scholarship football players and their institutional experience in higher education.* (2012: University of Southern California/pending)

**Mary** Zamon's letter included a "proposed process self-renewal model".

*Undergraduate critical thinking assessment processes and effects in a public university case study.* (2009: George Mason University)

**Carita** Harrell responds directly to the questions.

*Minority student success: A case study of the influence of spirituality on African-American student retention.* (2008: Arizona State University)

**Chad** Timm describes how data collection-analysis led him back to theory and forward to the development of his own.

*Circles of support: Towards a liberatory pedagogy for community education.* (2008: Iowa State University)

**Wanju** Huang describes using portraiture; Appendix III contains a brief description of her thesis connecting QR, children, and technology.

*Seeing the way they are in the way they IM: Case studies of Instant Messaging in Taiwanese fifth graders' lives.* (2010: University of Illinois, Urbana-Champaign)

**Karen** Hammel writes a candid letter related to the rationale for and experience of completing a self-study.

*Leadership preparation as one person's transformation: An ontology.* (2008: University of Minnesota, Minneapolis)

**Dennis** McCunney, a grad student at Morgan State University, provided the quotation that began our book.

**Sharon** Woodlief developed a methodology to work with her interests.

*Out of the classroom and into the heart of the matter: A case study of university student residents' reaction to access to muliticultural awareness education.* (2010: University of California, Santa Barbara)

**Bruce** Ingraham, a grad student at St. Mary's College of California, recommends we attend to "technology" – and so we did (although what is available to the readers since many of the correspondents completed their work is not described here)

**Jim** Barber (James P.), a former English language and literature major, extols the value of being part of a research team on a national project.

*Integration of learning: Meaning making for undergraduates through connection, application, and synthesis.* (2009: University of Michigan)

**Lisa** Heuvel's letter addresses major 'signposts' of the experience of QR and so became our "21st century table of contents".

*Teaching at the Interface: Curriculum and pedagogy in a teachers' institute on Virginia Indian history and cultures.* (2011: The College of William and Mary)

**Brighid** Dwyer, while a grad student, shares her already developed "hindsight".

*Students' cross-racial interactions at an emerging Hispanic-serving institution.* (2012: University of Michigan)

# ESTABLISHING A CONTEXT

**Jim B:** I have had some questions about classifying my work as qualitative or mixed methods.

## INTRODUCTION

Although one might think in the second decade of the 21st century that the thirty year old difficulty of "qualitative" *or* "quantitative" would have been silenced for good, the correspondents wrote that while learning about each *is* the current emphasis, the either/or/both questions remains something they were confronted with. My own ruminations about how best to present the correspondents' reflections led me to think about this issue as well. When I reviewed the focus questions and thought about the letters, I realized that some of what I learned could be summed up "in a nutshell." For example, question one asks: "How did you learn about qualitative research?" The simple answer to this question is that the correspondents learned about QR either during their undergraduate or master's programs, or heard about it for the first time early in their doctoral programs. Would a table, however, provide enough information to think with? Would a table help those new to QR grasp what it means to learn while doing? Does where the correspondents learned about it *tell* or merely *infer* the context of the experiences they had? I realized my "nutshell" was a faulty representation of the substance I was hoping for with my "how" (as opposed to "where") question. Providing more than an immediate answer *as well as* the "simplest" answer seems an appropriate strategy in a text designed to describe thinking while doing and demonstrate its complexity at every level. This is, therefore, the first reason I have chosen to share more, even if similar, "*tellings*" in Section One. A second reason for that decision is exemplified in **Rich**'s recollection, below. There is no way I might have anticipated his learning. Is it pertinent? Should I have left it out?

**Rich:** I learned about qualitative research from my grandmother, who passed about five years ago at the age of 97. I don't mean that to sound as corny as it does, but growing up in the South – conflicted place that it is – I learned a lot about how to talk to people from her. She was not always tactful; that is, she told people what they needed to hear, but only after spending time listening to what people told her. She talked to you as though you were the only person in the room, and a conversation with her was always a partnership. She wasn't waiting to say something, she was waiting to hear what you had to say. And she had a disarming lack of prejudicial expressions or intonations in the way that she talked, so that you felt like you could say anything. If I have a unique QR talent, it is the ability to talk to a wide variety of people, another quality that I learned from her.

Of course Rich's grandmother did not say to her five-year old grandson, "Now, Richie dear, I am going to tell you how to do qualitative research!" But when Rich began his formal research study, he realized that he had already acquired some skills and was living modeled behavior that qualitative researchers aspire to, e.g., observing, listening, rapport building, interacting easily with strangers. Rich describes the connection between a student's past experience and his current learning and understandings of QR, one of the themes across the letters.

A third reason a table alone would not suffice even as it seems to answer succinctly this most basic of questions is its inability to distinguish/differentiate among and across the learning experiences of the 69 correspondents in any way that allows for "transferability" (Lincoln & Guba, 1985). You, as readers, would have nothing to interpret, understand, or resonate to. Why do I want you to think of the correspondents beyond the fact that they were my "data set"? I could simply undertake frequency counts as to who did what, where, how – and for how long – and have, perhaps, an article? Would it be worth reading? If you think so, how would such a data set inform the *experiencing* of *your* learning? Does providing answers only, rather than "food for thought" promote or stymie your own thinking? Thinking is work. If you do undertake QR for your thesis, then you must be willing to do that work. Although a table might enable a succinct synopsis of "doing", it does not illuminate the choices and decision making involved. Including both – a few direct answers as well as amplification filled with detail, nuance, and yes, some redundancy – increases the probability (and I choose that word consciously!) that you, the reader, will take something away from these writings that matters to *you*. Sometimes we want just the facts; they help with decision making. Sometimes we want to know what others have thought and done – and again, this information also helps with decision making. None of us makes sense of material the same way. The conclusions you draw from these pages will become *your* understanding, *your* sense, and will therefore "stick" with you. I hope that as you get to know the correspondents, their ideas will inform, challenge, and support you. Like a hearty breakfast of slow carbs on a cold winter's morning, their reflections do have staying power!

Most importantly, then, a final reason for offering the explicit answers to the first, second and sixth focus questions has more to do with providing you with "food for thought" than serving you a singular, premeasured dose of what I choose to tell you, of the sense I think you "should" make. We hope you will use this book to help you do *your* work. You will decide when you have read enough. You will determine how much, or how little, and whose reflections inform you. With your colleagues and professors, you will interrogate the responses and the thinking and doing, coming to your own conclusions, just as the correspondents' writing links their decision making to their personal biography. Detailed indices by subject and correspondent conclude the book and may help this process.

A final rationale, if I need one, for providing more information than you might want to read or think you need to know is to offer students and professors substantive material with which to examine what it is you are doing compared to others. I am not talking about being able to generalize experience; I am talking about learning from it, as I have done with the correspondence I received. The correspondents are with me, encouraging me to be an ever wiser professor, a more aware colleague, and a gentler friend.

# QUALITATIVE AND QUANTITATIVE

**Jim B:** For one part of my analysis, I counted the number of examples in each of the three main categories and correlated these data with the participants' developmental levels, which had been assessed on a 10-point scale by an in-depth study of the interview data. I have been told after the fact that this process of "quantitizing" qualitative data could actually classify my dissertation as "mixed methods" because I mixed my data at the analysis stage (Creswell & Plano Clark, 2011). However, I have not considered my work to be mixed methods because all of the original data were qualitative (personal interviews). In fact, I was not aware of the concept (or even the term!) of "quantitizing" until after my dissertation was completed and defended.

## INTRODUCTION

One of the first things I learned about my twenty-first century correspondents was that undergraduate students were learning about qualitative research and masters' students are using it to complete their theses. I also discovered more than several contributors are non-native English speakers, and not all of them come from the field of education; nursing, music, and business come quickly to mind. When I think back about what I learned, when I learned it, and how I went about it, I can barely imagine what it must be like to accomplish that task in a language other than my own, or from a perspective foreign to my own. Although some graduate students might be sensitive to the "phd" or "edd" issue, I found what differentiated my correspondents one from the other was not their degree program, but rather the amount of time they had to give me and their proximity to an issue.

### QUESTION ONE: HOW DID YOU LEARN ABOUT QR?

Table 1 below does not directly answer the "how" question, but it will let you know at a glance how many correspondents focused on this question. It will give you some idea of where/when their learning took place.

*Table 1. Where/When Correspondents' Learned about QR*

| Program | Male | Female | N |
| --- | --- | --- | --- |
| Undergraduate | | 4 | 4 |
| Master's Program/Thesis | | 10 | 10 |
| Doctoral Program | 5 | 16 | 21 |
| Other | 1 | | 1 |
| Total | 6 | 30 | 36 |

*Note.* N=36 correspondents described specifics for this question.

> *The experiences of learning about qualitative research required more explanation. In order to provide some logic here, I have decided to begin with correspondents who learned about QR at the doctoral level, followed by masters' and undergraduate experiences. I begin with the opening of* **Shaunna**'s *letter and continue with the responses of her colleagues.*

During the fall semester of 2006, I found myself alongside 22 relatively 'green' doctoral students at our orientation weekend. We were an eclectic group, representing a large spectrum of fields and disciplines, from business administration to biology, from high school to higher education, from the social sciences to social work. Throughout the orientation weekend, we were bombarded with various forms of the same question from faculty, staff, current students, and alumni alike: "What is your proposed dissertation topic?" "What is your area of study?" "Do you know what you want to research?" As a naïve yet consistent overachiever and first-generation college student, I originally proposed (in front of God and everybody) that I planned to conduct a mixed-methodology dissertation concerning the spiritual development of college students. Little did I know there were already two major challenges to my academic goal. First, the formulation of methodology should *follow* the research questions rather than *precede* them (Light, Singer & Willett, 1990), and second, there was an entire team of researchers who were already studying *my* topic. In hindsight, clearly my plan was overambitious, under-researched, and did not make sense to a logical, educated thinker.

I continued to embrace my original topic, having no idea how much it, my identities, and my life would change as a result of writing a QD. Whenever I ran to my dissertation chairperson for guidance and advice, he drove home the point, "Whatever makes sense!" There were so many concerns that did not make sense while attempting to pull together my first (AND LAST!) dissertation project. I spent a lot of time on my own thinking, researching, and writing in ways that needed to make sense, both to myself and to the outside world of scholars who would critique, and hopefully use my final study.

There were several priorities that helped me make sense of my experience writing a QD. I have highlighted four: choosing a topic (p. 36), positionality (p. 117), the importance of language (p. 120), and finally doing "Whatever makes sense!" (p. 128). Tackling these issues directly contributed to my persistence during the pre-candidacy phase, the completion of the dissertation, the defense hearing during the candidacy phase, and the impact of my QD project post-graduation given a healthy dose of intellectual freedom.

**Corey** knew absolutely nothing about QR. I taught math and science, so I was more intent on quant research. **Julie**, as a math teacher, had always been so focused on quant research. Although I have taken a QR class, I actually feel like I am stronger at quant than qual, but QR fits better with the subject I have chosen to investigate.

**Jim O**'s first QR course took place during the second term of my doctoral program.

**Mary**'s program required three introductory research methods courses: intro (mostly an overview of quant), a quant, a qual, and one advanced course, which in my case was Program Evaluation. My qual instructor went through basic methodologies but did not address much the qual/quant or mixed methods discussion. I was okay on tools but not concepts.

**Tom** had research classes in quant, qual, and mixed methods research. It was an intense learning curve to experience all three types of research at the beginning of the program.

**Isabelle** was introduced to QR through a class on research methods in applied linguistics. While QR was rigorous, it was not about numbers. I realized I wanted to tell stories. Quant research lacks the human factor. I was investigating stereotypes; statistics/quant was not the way to go.

**Wanju**'s educational background prepared me for quant types of research. Because I believed I would be more comfortable working with numbers/statistics, I started taking courses that would help me understand and conduct quant research. However, my adviser and several of the professors tended to use QR methods in their research. I began to take and audit QR courses such as Action Research, Mixed Methods, Case Study, etc., even though I doubted I had the vocabulary of QR in me. In those courses, I was exposed to different types of studies that required me to conduct interviews, write field notes, analyze interview data, and report research findings in a QI fashion.

**Joan** took a course on qual case methods, which was my formal introduction to the major components of QR. Prior to this course, most of the emphasis was on quant research, especially in the Stat I and II courses. **Ellie** was able to take research methods courses from well-known scholars at her university, "the Mecca of QR".

**Katherine**'s program was quite rigorous, requiring 18 hours of research coursework. I started with the basic epistemology course called, "Foundations of

Human Inquiry" and then took the "Intro to Quantitative" followed by the "Intro to Qualitative" research courses. Additional course work and independent study included: "Integrating Quant and Qual Methods"; "Ethnography"; "Feminist Theory"; "Feminist Ethnography"; and, "Historical and Archival Methods".

**Francesca** feels lucky that several professors in my department primarily use QM in their own research. The department highlights QR publications and presentations, making it seem as important as quant research. In addition, I was assigned as a research assistant to a professor who works in mixed methods. She included me in several long term research projects, training me in methods such as focus groups, field observation, participant observation, open-ended survey analysis, and interviewing.

**Jim B** learned about QR by doing it! I do not recall having a sense of qual vs. quant research when I began my doctoral program. I had the great fortune to be offered an opportunity with a national research study as a first year doc student, an assistantship I maintained throughout my doctoral work. I learned about QR philosophy and methodology, gained data collection skills, e.g., interviewing, and had extensive practice analyzing qual data.

The principal investigators (PIs), two faculty members, led the QR portion. They had expertise in QR and provided training sessions for the research team, which were as important to my development as a qual researcher as any of my formal coursework. The PIs also provided excellent mentoring, challenging research assignments, and writing opportunities for the students involved. Both eventually served on my dissertation committee, one as the chair.

After a year of experience, I conducted my own QR project as an independent study. It allowed me to use the skills I had gained and afforded experience with research design. For this project, I was the one making decisions about participant recruitment, sample size, interview protocol, and member checking.

I also took three QM courses: *Qualitative Methods in Educational Research, Introduction to Discourse Analysis,* and *Assessing Self-Authorship.* Each provided a variety of approaches, allowing me to learn from three different faculty members with distinct research agendas and styles.

*By now I hope you are beginning to realize that the synthesis answer* Table 1 *provides does little to get at the differences in courses, background experiences, and opportunities the term "learning" connotes.*

Many years ago, **Sharon** began my graduate program in a department that focused on quant methodology. I transferred and found that approach continued. The degree requirements were unfulfilling, kind of a "repeat"; there was no QR requirement. Finally, in the school of education, I found coursework that included qual and quant methodology. From that first course, I felt the possibilities of doing research and contributing to the field of education blossom.

For someone like **Cassandra** with an educational and professional background in business, seeking a Ph.D. in educational leadership was definitely a stretch outside of my comfort zone and area of expertise. Therefore, to write a dissertation, I knew I had to follow an approach I was comfortable with. My profession deals with asking a lot of open-ended questions and then writing projects and procedures for various end-user groups. While numbers are important, they do not convey the message that a detailed report can. By the end of my first research class, weighing out the merits of qual versus quant research, I had already decided I would conduct a QS. I knew I could discover a story and tell it. I just didn't know, from a scholarly perspective, how structured and rigorous my work had to be.

Due to the nature and structure of the three year program I was in, there was very little time to become adequately acquainted with the various forms of QR. I only remember taking one formal qual class in addition to the introductory class; this brief exposure was not enough to teach or prepare a person for QR. Thus, I sought advice and looked for resources outside of my department. I talked to friends who had completed qual dissertations. I read articles pulled from ProQuest about QM. I even contacted some of the researchers whose qual studies I read. I actually spoke to one researcher who told me to immerse myself in the literature on QR for a number of different genres, even if I was not interested in the topic area, to get exposure to and explore various qual designs and writing styles.

*To synthesize, then, those who told me they were introduced/learned QR at the doctoral level include*: Shaunna, Corey, Julie, Jim O, Mary, Tom, Isabelle, Wanju, Joan, Ellie, Katherine, Francesca, Jim B, Sharon and Cassandra. **Grover** shares his story, below.

My journey with QR started with an innocent comment from my mentor. While discussing my dissertation, he off-handedly asked if I had considered QR, specifically phenomenological research. I say the comment was off-handed because he did not wait for my answer, and I did not offer one at the time. I had not done much studying in QR prior to his comment and was unsure if this would be a good option for my research. I spent the next few days looking up this great research method and reading books by Creswell (1998; 2005) and Moustakas (1994). The topic for my dissertation was the emotional impact felt by instructors for Air Force basic military training and how these emotions affected their ability to train. After reading as much information as possible I realized a phenomenological study was the best option for my research, and maybe my mentor's comment was not as off-handed as I thought. Exploring the lived experiences of these men and women would be more enriching and data filled if I allow them to express their shared experiences. I contacted my mentor and my journey with QR took off.

The first debate with my dissertation committee was when to accomplish the literature review. There are times in this type of research when we will accomplish the LR last so as not to provide any pre-conceived notions about the study. This debate was the first of several issues one of my committee members had with the process of my research. We ultimately decided to conduct the LR prior to the study but added a detailed section to the dissertation in chapter four (Epoche) about my experiences and thoughts on the subject. This section allowed me to provide any thoughts or experiences I had with regard to my subject. My mentor and committee accepted this version of the dissertation and my research flourished.

The biggest obstacle for my dissertation was the final submission of Chapter 4. My mentor and I agreed that this chapter should read like a novel, an in-depth story of the lives of the research participants. This narrative flowed like a conversation to enrich the delivery of as much data as possible; there was a significant amount of first person. One of my committee members was adamant that first person not be allowed anywhere in the dissertation. My mentor and I talked with her and showed her the references allowing first person in the narrative form of this type of research. Ultimately my mentor asked the Dean of my college, a qualitative researcher, to look at the document and determine the validity of my use of first person. With this done the one committee member grudgingly agreed to my final product if I added a section to explain how my results married to every topic in the literature review. This part of the process proved to be wonderful because it added another level of validity to my research as my findings and the findings of studies in the literature review were consistent.

I had always considered myself a traditionalist in studies and research. I am profoundly grateful for my mentor opening my eyes to a type of research I would have never considered. Best wishes, Grover.

*Across the next few pages*, Amanda, Jessie, Isabeau, Ginny, Sandy, *and* Monica Jean *relate that their first QR learning experience occurred during their masters'* *programs.*

**Amanda** first learned about QR in my MEd program. My professors would always point out if a study was qual or quant; I was perplexed. My truer understanding came when I took my QR methods course; I instantly felt free. I was particularly drawn to grounded theory study but ultimately would discover and utilize an untested, proposed method identified as a way to synthesize more than 4 or 5 qual studies called "Meta-Interpretation" (Weed, 2005; 2008).

When working on **Jessie**'s master's, my advisor suggested a mixed method study. As a doctoral student, I struggled with deciding to repeat the mixed methods approach. My qual core course provided the ground work for realizing that my interest would be best suited for QI; an advanced qual course worked through the advantages, disadvantages and best fit applicability of several methods.

Most of **Isabeau**'s initial learning came from doing the process myself in my MA; developing interview questions, recruiting and interviewing participants, transcribing, coding by hand, etc. I took a course on feminist methodology and on qual data analysis before I got to a point, just at the tail end of completing my proposal, where I thought: "OMG, I don't know what I'm doing!" With recruitment and interviews around the corner, not to mention the daunting task of analysis,

I realized I needed further help. So I took a 1-term qual data analysis course in my department, which also helped. In a way, it also shot down any smidge of confidence I might have had because the course reinforced that a QR approach is anything but "cookie cutter."

**Ginny**'s first experiences of QR occurred when I was working on my master's degree. I remember looking through educational theses for a research project, noticing all the tables and charts and feeling discouraged about having to read and interpret all of that data. Then I came upon a qual thesis! It contained neither tables nor data driven charts with statistics embedded in the text. It was like a story almost; I could read through it without having to stop every paragraph or two to re-read the material in order to make sense of it. It was really interesting; I could understand and relate to what I was reading. The connections to the participants and the research questions were clear. The writing was clearer, academic certainly but with a sense of personal, hands-on authenticity that was somehow lacking in the quant research. I knew then I wanted to conduct my study like that.

**Sandy** also used QR in her master's thesis in 1995. I have since taken several QR courses including Methods in QR, Case Study Research and Program Evaluation.

**Monica Jean**'s first major QS was my master's thesis. At the time I conducted the study I had a very basic understanding of QR. As I continued into a Ph.D. program, so did my interest in utilizing QM, because I want to understand *why* things are the way they are. I am interested in the stories people have to tell, in the rich data that QR allows.

*QR is no longer limited to a few graduate students in masters' and doctoral programs.* Anabella, Megan, Angela LV, *and* Amy *write about their learning at the undergraduate level.*

When **Anabella** and colleagues approached our professor with the idea for our undergraduate thesis project, he suggested QR as the best way to address it. Undertaking it provided me with important insight into QR from start to finish.

Through **Megan**'s undergraduate and graduate experiences, I felt that numbers – always a strong suit of mine – never really told the whole story. I was drawn to learning about new topics by reading and pursuing QS in my undergraduate and graduate course work.

**Angela LV** first learned about QR when I was an undergraduate student in my home country Colombia, South America, where I majored in foreign language education – English and French – at a public university in the early 90s. In one class during the fourth year of my program, I was assigned to read one research article and to report on it. In the city where I lived, there was a Colombian-US binational cultural center, well known for its English courses, its cultural programs, and its library, which was always updated with the latest in books, movies, music, and research journals in the area of language teaching. I became familiar with a major journal in my area (TESOL journal), which mainly published quant articles.

Without previous exposure to published research reports, and with no instruction on how to make sense of this kind of academic text, reading these articles was an overwhelming endeavor. Understanding them was a daunting task, with the added difficulty of reading in my still developing second language.

In the late 1990s, we started hearing about "action research". A nation-wide research project on language teaching programs in the country was taking place. One of my favorite professors was a participant. As her student, I had first-hand information about the project. I remember her excitement; her passion for it was contagious. In her class we read several action research reports. One aspect that caught my attention was that I could connect to the writing and understand the "stories" embedded in it. I did not feel the frustration I felt when reading the "other" research articles I had been assigned to read without support. The new research articles felt like reading about real life; it was quite inspirational.

Very quickly, we started thinking about ideas to conduct action research projects during our student-teaching assignment. Innocently, many of us thought that writing up our reports would be easy, and that the fluidity of the writing we found in the articles we read was going to come up in our reports right from the start! Well, it took very little time for us all to realize that writing up our research reports required a vast amount of knowledge and writing skills. The passion and enthusiasm for telling our found classroom "stories" proved insufficient when confronted with the challenge of producing a decent, readable written report.

In retrospect, I now understand that one of the major accomplishments of qual researchers who get to publish their work is that they make it look "easy" to the untrained reader. After many years of graduate work and intensive QR training, I now fully understand that what fired up my interest in "that other type of research" was the result of wisely crafting and articulating a great deal of insight, knowledge, and experience on paper. For me, that was and still is one of the most challenging aspects of conducting QR.

**Amy** learned about QR in an undergraduate communications class; I was fascinated by the amount of detail. The stories were meaningful and stuck with me because of the way they were told; the readings didn't feel like work, they felt like I was meeting people.

*One of the many things you may have noticed across the responses so far is that 21st century correspondents learned by doing.* Roxanne *contributes both the first and last excerpt under the topic of "assignments", below, with* Bruce, Donna, Rich, Vic, Kristan, *and* Michele *sharing their thoughts in between.*

ASSIGNMENTS – OR NOT?

When **Roxanne** was a graduate student, I never felt I had experience analyzing my own data and presenting those results. So structuring the narrative was difficult for me. It's like you have so much you want to say, or you think is important, and you have limited to space to say it.

**Bruce** has an MA in mathematics and a day job as a marketing science consultant. Every course in my doctoral program required a small QR project. One was in QM for math education research. I also worked as a graduate research assistant on projects that used QM.

**Donna** remembers thinking the day I first heard about QR at the beginning of my doctoral coursework that it was such a perfect fit for me. One of the assignments was to craft a mini-proposal. As a public school teacher, I was concerned about factors contributing to the low numbers of women in Science, Technology, Engineering, and Math (STEM) programs. My daughters had taken higher level STEM courses and were often the only females in the class. During my master's program, the assigned readings included Michael Apple, Joe Kincheloe, and Paulo Freire. While developing a LR, I seemed to be drawn to critical studies with qual designs, as though they spoke to me and my experiences.

Anyway, in the course of gathering information, reading, developing the proposal, and discussing all of this with my family, a heated disagreement drastically changed the path of my dissertation study. My interest emanated from the provocations of my son during an argument about women in male-dominated STEM careers. He posited that it is more difficult for men to enter a sex role specific occupation than for a woman to do the same. After watching the movie, *Meet the Parents*, my son was dismayed at the disrespectful portrayal of Ben Stiller's character who was a man in nursing. My then teen-aged son challenged me to investigate men in nursing and see if their experiences mirrored that of women in the STEM careers. I accepted his dare and was shocked to find a scarcity of information about men in female-dominated, sex role specific, professions. There were smatterings of qual studies concerning men in teaching, administrative assistants, and librarians, and a few, exceptional studies about men in nursing.

I am not a nurse. I am a woman, middle-aged with grown children. I was an outsider looking into a world that was far removed from my experiences. I felt as though I could only conduct this type of research through QM because they provided a vibrant means to allow the participants to respond in their own voice.

**Rich** took a series of courses on QR, including a module each on focus groups and interviewing. But, as an experiential learner, there is no substitute for *the doing* of QR; and so, I sought out as many experiences as I could to actually do interviews and, later, focus groups. I had conducted approximately 150 interviews by the time I completed my dissertation work. I sought out academics, university administrators, business professionals, service station owners (more on those later), farmers, public officials, and others to interview. This range of interviewees came through research experiences with multiple professors across multiple departments, and through my own additional research that I conducted in addition to student-professor projects.

This range of experiences broke down a lot of barriers for me in terms of choosing a dissertation topic. Your range of workable research questions gets a lot wider when you aren't intimidated or restricted by access issues, or catalogued difficulties among certain populations in the research literature. One of the research populations that I chose – service station owners – are not even present in the QR literature.

Around the time of concluding **Vic**'s prospectus, I conducted two pilot case studies. HIGHLY RECOMMENDED! Pilots solve a lot of issues in terms of interview questions, potential coding approaches (Auerbach & Silverstein, 2006) and emergent themes. When you begin your actual research, you can achieve greater focus.

As a first generation college student, **Kristan** really did not know the difference between qual and quant until I began my doctoral program. Part of why I decided to proceed with doctoral work was because of my interest in hearing and sharing the experiences of low income students and students of color as they transition from high school to college.

Formally, I learned about the mechanics of QR by doing it and reading qual studies. Some of the most influential ones were Patricia Gandara's *Over the Ivy Walls*, Patricia McDonough's *Choosing colleges: How social class and schools structure inequality*, Ana Castillo's *Massacre of the Dreamers* and Angela Valenzuela's *Subtractive Schooling*. Each of these examples are dissertations that later became books.

Informally, I am very inspired by film, autobiography, and other non-fiction. I started to watch the Paul Almond's 7UP films during my dissertation writing. They heavily influenced how I thought about depicting the narrative of another, especially in thinking about how individual stories develop over time. I think that being able to "see" the stories of other as a snapshot of their overall life has helped me to think about QR in a different way.

In **Michele**'s first semester I took an introduction to research class, wherein we explored quant, qual, and historical research methodologies. For each section we completed a "mini paper". I remember reading Tom Barone's (1993) "Ways of Being at Risk: The Case of Billy Charles Barnett." I found it to be more artistic than I thought research could be, a more personal approach and more in line with how I viewed individuals as unique. I also thought it looked easier than research that used numbers. Boy, was I wrong!

**Roxanne** first learned about QR in the first two semesters of my doctoral program. Although neither was a QM class, I read a number of qual studies. The one that demonstrated the important contribution of QR was Willis' *Leaning to Labor*. I particularly liked his descriptions, which spoke to my own observations regarding the distribution of power in schools.

> **Nancy** *provides one of the most memorable examples of an early assignment,*
> *below, bringing the experience of "learning by doing" to life.*

When I was finishing my Master's program, the chair of my thesis committee invited me to take a QR class. I had written my thesis using quant measures and had little exposure to QM, so I wasn't sure if this was a class I wanted to take. Also, I had heard from several faculty members that QR wasn't a legitimate form of research. I thought I might be wasting time and a credit.

I decided to take the class, however, when I needed another statistics credit and because the class was offered in the summer. Our first assignment was to find an unusual place to do a QS, one that would provide rich, descriptive data. It just so happened that a summer festival was going on in my hometown, and I knew there would be a carnival. I decided this location was where I wanted to do my research.

The first day I walked around taking notes, trying to gather descriptive data. My plan was to interview people who were attending the carnival. I was going to ask them if they rode the carnival rides, why they rode the rides, and if they didn't, why they chose not to—were they afraid? However, as I walked around taking notes, I noticed carnival workers began slipping back into the shadows. After a few minutes of this, a gruff looking gentleman stopped me and asked, "Are you with the cops? Or maybe you're an inspector? What are you doing writing stuff down in the notebook?"

I looked at his missing teeth and burnt leather skin and immediately made the assumption that I was about to be pulled behind a semi-truck and knifed. I responded that I wasn't the law or an inspector and that I was just doing research for a class. He replied, "Well, you know, people around here get nervous when they see people taking notes."

I asked him why I made them nervous; he said that "town people" always make assumptions about "carnies." He said that that carnies were no different than anyone else—they fell in love, got married, made babies, and buried their dead in cemeteries, just like other folks. He added that people on the outside think carnies are all thieves, prostitutes, murderers, perverts, alcoholics, and drug addicts. He said that he had a wife, two sons, and a nice home back in Texas. He joined the carnival when he was about 17-years-old and loved it. He spends nine months out of the year on the road, and he gets to stay home with his family in the winter. He said he made enough from his carnival game not to have to work any other jobs all year – and then he pointed to the bright new semi that was parked beside his canopy. "That is mine – bought and paid for – so is my house. And I got money in the bank to send my kids to college," he said. He added, "If you look at me you wouldn't think I was nothing but a bum – my hair ain't been cut in a month, and I ain't had a bath in three days. I been standing in this sun for 16 hours a day since March. I gotta right to look like I do."

I asked if I could interview him for my research, and he said yes; he seemed flattered that I would want to talk to him. I asked if there was anyone else who would want to talk to me, and he grabbed four other people: a young cotton candy vendor who was barely out of high school; an old man who ran the Ferris wheel and had been with the carnival for some 50 years; and a woman and her husband who had pretty much been born into the profession. It was while talking to these "carnies" that I grew to love QR.

*As I near ending this section, I offer a contribution from* **Brighid**, *who begins using the phrase, "In hindsight." I noticed this phrase and a second one, "in the end", across more than several of the letters. These phrases seemed to signal a consolidating thought, in a form slightly different than direct ADVICE, which also appears throughout this book. See what you think!*

In hindsight, I wish I had known what resources were available on campus and had taken advantage of them. For example, I took a class with a notable qual researcher in a different academic department, but only after the fact came to find out that her methods were not as valued in my discipline. For another, I knew there was a well-known qual researcher in my school, but the main method she used was not the method I was planning on using, so I did not take her class. Later I discovered the skills students learned in her class were very transferrable; no doubt taking her course probably would have been very useful. I also discovered later she was a huge advocate for students.

CONCLUSION

In the introduction to this book, I suggested that qualitative researchers often come to their notion of themes and pertinent issues through some sort of understanding of emphasis, e.g., by a physically observed reaction across participants or a frequency count of an issue. I introduced this section with the thinking of **Jim B** (p. 17), who expressed concern about what to "call" his study. Data, whether numbers or words, are the pieces of information we use to make sense of our focus. These data, arrived at through no a priori intention to count or place into predetermined categories, remain "qualitative"? That I can discover nominal and ordinal data in and across responses and illuminate this information using numbers or tables means I am thinking while doing, working with the riches – and richness – of my data set? To not notice or to do less would only illuminate a blind spot in the workings of "the human instrument" and underestimate (another quant word?) my!/our? capacity to comprehend at a variety of levels of data analysis? If I am not mistaken, a mixed methods study infers intent; I enter the study ready to count and ready to describe. In this study, I realized there was a story to be told with tables and counts within a book about "thinking while doing" and thereby decided to create them to illuminate and make succinct the experiencing of my correspondents while making visible the limitations of this form of data display. Analysis is complex and multi-layered/leveled. I will now read Creswell and Plano Clark (2011) to be sure I understand what Jim B is talking about. All error in understanding and interpretation is mine, as I am still learning while doing!

Prior to presenting summative Table 2, below, I would like to conclude Part One of Section One with a suggestion **Mary** makes, one I suspect is already occurring in IHEs around the world.

I feel compelled to say that in general there is still a lingering culture at the university…that QR is not "real" because it is not generalizable. My experience with both tells me that qualitative is HARDER and answers the how and why questions in a much better way. It is the good combination of quant AND qual methods that can provide deep answers to important research questions and problems faced today. A utopian idea is to have a team of researchers with multiple methodologies work collectively on a research problem.

*Table 2. Numbers vs Rich Description: Where Correspondents Learned about Rich Description*

|  | *Quantitative Reply* | *Qualitative Reply* |
| --- | --- | --- |
| Word Count | 37 | 4677 |
| Pages | 1 | 10 |

# QUALITATIVE OR QUANTITATIVE

**Rich:** I love numbers but have never believed that they tell the most complete story. Many policy (and otherwise) mistakes have been carried out under the guise that numbers are either "the truth," or that we ought to work towards the truth that only they can project. With that said, one of the four manuscripts in my dissertation is comprised mostly of…numbers. Yes, it also includes qual descriptors of phenomena that help to build context and tell a story about those numbers; but primarily, it is numbers. This question, qual vs quant, seems often to come down to numbers, and whether it makes sense to use them, or whether a student, or faculty member for that matter, prefers them.

I believe that when we abstract away from individual stories and their nuances, we lose the ability to offer people meaningful solutions. Abstraction results in a diminished ability for solutions to be relatable; if we aren't offering people anything, why are we academics?

## INTRODUCTION

With the second focus question the correspondents' narratives began to develop, helping me acquire both a sense of each contributor as an individual human being and the thinking he/she was doing early in the research process. Twenty-first century correspondents are strong learners, providing knowledgeable responses to what might seem like a 'feels good' question.

## QUESTION TWO: WHY DID YOU CHOOSE QR?

Table 3, below, can be regarded either as the key ideas across the remaining pages of Part Two or as an introduction to it. I will then continue with a second excerpt from **Shaunna**, not only to keep her story going but also to immediately explore the personal history – decision making connection.

*Table 3. Correspondents' Rationale for Choosing QR*

| Reasoning | Male | Female |
|---|---|---|
| QR made sense for the questions I am asking | 2 | 4 |
| Quant did not answer the questions I had | 1 | 2 |
| QR captures stories of marginalized groups | 1 | 1 |
| To tell the story I want to know more about | | 3 |
| I was at grad school to learn what I did not know | 1 | |
| An interest in methodology and a professor's suggestion | | 2 |
| No literature in the area of study | | 1 |
| Because the literature is full of quant studies | | 1 |
| Quant doesn't address my biases or subjects' stories | | 1 |
| The rich descriptive data | | 1 |
| Knew from the start | | 2 |
| QR "fits" me | | 2 |
| QR made more sense | | 1 |
| It is important that participants feel comfortable enough to share | 1 | |
| We need to offer people meaningful solutions | 1 | |
| Because of the location of responsibility in QR | | 1 |
| I almost did not have a choice | 1 | |
| TOTALS | 8 | 22 |

*Note.* N=30 correspondents described specifics for this question.

**Shaunna**'s Priority One: Choose a topic that lends itself to *QR*! Going into my weekend cohort-formatted doctoral program, I demanded the fast track. There were so many other endeavors I wanted to pursue that I decided to dedicate approximately three years solely to professional and academic endeavors just to push through in an uninterrupted fashion. I did not know this estimated time-to-completion was almost impossible to accomplish. Regardless, I had committed members in my accountability group who were also ready, willing, and definitely intellectually able to stay on such a fast track alongside me, since we began with similar expectations of the program.

A number of colleagues chose dissertation topics that were quant in nature, which initially seemed to guarantee lightning-fast time to completion yet were not personally fulfilling investments of their time, energy, and tuition. It seemed odd and inauthentic to choose topics that were of high interest to a dissertation chair, yet not the student.

I called my topic – the spiritual development of lesbian, gay, and bisexual (LGB) students – the ultimate oxymoron to who I was as a researcher, because it had everything to do with my spiritual interests as a trained campus minister yet little to do with my personal identity as a heterosexual female. As a perceived outsider to LGB communities, I became vested in seeking out and listening to the experiences of these silenced communities as I became more familiar with the oppression they incurred regularly. I deeply wanted to conduct my study out of both personal and professional interest, that is, the "want-to-do-ability" (Marshall and Rossman, 1999) that connects research to life experiences (p. 10). By conducting my study, I was able to further explain a phenomenon in depth. This ability emerged directly from who I was at the time of the study, and overwhelmingly developed who I am now as an ally to LBG communities. It was up to me to determine how quickly I proceeded, what elements were essential, and which projects could wait. I can say that I conducted my own study on my own terms.

*As you will read in the selections below, choosing QR is a personal decision based on a number of factors. For* Amy, Jim O, Katherine, *and others, the "fit" seems "natural."*

**Amy** wants the answer to the questions quant research raises for me. Behind every outlier, every number, there is a story. I want to know what the stories are. I don't care if 88% of students can answer a question. I want to see the process, how they solve the problem.

As an elementary teacher, I often see claims made by various programs about their effectiveness. I have always wanted to know what sorts of students each program was effective for? Would it work for my kids? Was it best suited for a certain group, or would it work equally well for all kids under all circumstances? These questions were never answered and made me realize that while quant studies give a nice overview of a problem, I wanted the depth that qualitative studies provide.

During my experiences in qual and quant research classes, **Jim O** quickly realized that I was more qualitatively "bent." My research areas of interest relate to marginalized groups, identity development, and life histories. As I read more and more research, it became clear to me that QR played a key role in capturing the stories of these individuals while enabling the reader to better understand what life or an experience is like for them.

**Katherine** knew from the start that my dissertation would be qualitative. It just fits with my personality and my strengths. I am a "people person" not a "number cruncher."

*Recognizing the value of QR in* exploring complex and ambiguous phenomena **Kj** *adds*: QR fits with what I was seeking to find, but it is also a part of who I am. I really connected with the epistemology and purpose of QR. I am more interested in developing a deep understanding of some phenomenon than being able to create broad generalizations about a topic.

**Kristan** chose QM because it seemed natural to tell the story that I wanted to know more about – how low income Latinas understand their pathways to college using financial aid. These stories would have been difficult to capture in any other way.

**Julie, Carita**, and **Jim B** *write that* QR was the best choice for [their] research questions. It allows **Isabeau** to examine the questions I have in a way that is most useful to my research interests. **Bruce** *agrees*: The method follows from the research question within the context of the theoretical framework; my question requires QM.

*Some of the correspondents are self-identified "quants", such as* Vic *and* Francesca, *below. For them, QR was not "natural". It took some learning by doing for* Ronn *to grasp QR's potential.*

**Vic** was interested in QM because my previous training and limited research experience had been more quantitative. I was in the doctoral program to learn; given the opportunities that existed, I should learn the qual approach instead of taking the easier way out, which, in our cohort, appeared to be quant survey research. Most cohort members, in the end, realized that QR could be much more difficult than a quant approach, and be invaluable in investigating complex issues, particularly education. **Francesca** has experience with statistics and statistical analysis, however, I found that QR offered some opportunities that stats do not.

**Ronn** initially began graduate school with an interest in quant research. As such, I was paired with an advisor who was an economist. I had the opportunity to participate in research focused on how schools made decisions about using resources. My role involved meeting with principals to collect their responses to a detailed survey about resource allocation. The project was important; however, I found the data collection process did not answer the questions I had.

During my second year of graduate school I began working with a professor who conducted QR in urban areas. I was drawn to case study and life history research that captured the experiences of people and how experiences changed over time. My only concern was that I had left teaching elementary school because I thought that research had the potential to inform practice and improve the educational opportunities of underserved students. I assumed that only large scale quant research could achieve this end. To my surprise, the research I was involved in contextualized how the lived experiences of individuals inform policy creation and implementation. We presented our work at conferences and in journals. The depth of QR helped people understand how students experienced the educational process.

> *As I read the letters related to this question, the methodological interest of several caught my attention, e.g.,* Megan, Amanda, Mary, *and* Jessie, *as well as* Tiffany, Anabella, *and* anonymous. *I placed* Cindy's *response in the middle of these in order to connect the attention to methodology to a particular context.*

Most of **Megan**'s classmates entered the program knowing exactly what they wanted the end result to look like; I was pretty sure of my research methodology only. I wanted to do something that would make a difference in practice – and in the lives of the college students with whom I worked. When I stepped back after several classes to reflect on what I had done thus far, I realized that my papers, projects, and discussions all centered around a common thread; I realized I was getting closer to my topic.

**Amanda** chose the meta-interpretation method because it was something I understood, and it was untested; QR was also a better match for my learning style.

**Mary**'s courses whetted my appetite for methodology in general – a very unexpected turn of interest. I did feel more at home with QM or as I later found out, mixed methods. I have taken to heart some advice St. Thomas gives, "beware of absolutes" and so lean to mixing. I assume some of this predilection comes from my background as a history teacher, as well as my first degrees in Foreign Service, which had three 'majors' – history, economics and politics.

The professor in research design also inspired my curiosity and wonder about a new idea, i.e., one could alter and improve the research methods as one went along! Wow! New thoughts, but not so easy to apply!

**Jessie** wanted to add a new dimension and depth to the existing quant studies. QI also provides space and time for stories to percolate up. I enjoy existing in that nexus of time between the asking of a question and hearing the response – it is in those precious seconds when a person is committing themselves to you, deciding to trust you with what is precious to them – their story. QI also allows me to challenge my own perceptions and beliefs.

**Cindy** wanted my dissertation to tell the story of the Vietnamese community college. The subjects, if properly selected, were the experts. I was not. The subjects understood their culture, which was foreign to me, an American who had never visited Viet Nam prior to 2007. I was biased. Born in the middle of the U.S. in 1960, Viet Nam was a war, not a nation. Even though I spent three years reading everything I could about the country, and making two visits prior to my research to develop relationships in a communal and relationship-based culture, I still wasn't an "expert" on Viet Nam. I was not socialized in the culture. I was an outsider; even more importantly, I was a biased outsider whose society had waged war against the people I wanted to study. I had been socialized through the institutions of family, politics and education to view the Vietnamese as communist who could not be trusted. Neither my biases nor the subjects' stories would be addressed in a quantitative study.

**Tiffany** chose QR because I found it easy to become engrossed in learning about it. However, it was not at all easy to learn how to do it – or to actually start doing it!

**Anabella,** knowing I wanted to undertake QR, chose a dissertation advisor who had a significant scholarly trajectory in QR. The combination of my work with students in an advisory capacity, my desire to understand their needs and perspectives, and my previous experience with a QR project let me to pursue it at the doctoral level.

**ANON** almost did not have a choice. It seemed as if the professors in the program pushed in the qual direction. …. The nice thing about making the decision to be a qual researcher, however, is that I was surrounded by some of the best qual researchers in the country.

*The passage from* **Debra**'s *letter below makes explicit many of the connecting threads across the reflections of others, from how she learned and who she was to what she was thinking and learning as she continued her studies.*

Why I Chose Qualitative Research for my Dissertation.   Using a qual approach for my dissertation was the result of all the research I conducted before even getting to that stage, as well as my own personal story. When I entered the doctoral program, I was a "nontraditional" student in that I was middle-aged, had been working in low-wage jobs, and had only recently returned to school to even finish my bachelor's degree. Perhaps because I was older, I initially worried that I was "out of my league" and would not be able to successfully complete the doctoral program.

Qualitative Methods I was my very first doctoral class. My research project focused on the perceptions of six child care teachers as they struggled to meet the demands of our state's BA mandate. I found that not only did the teachers and I have a lot in common, but they were so grateful to have their concerns and issues voiced. In addition, by giving a voice to their perceptions, my work had the potential to inform larger quant research studies, and in turn, state policy. I found this combination quite fulfilling on both a personal and professional level and ended up focusing on QR in almost all of the work leading up to my dissertation.

Angela LV *goes beyond a simple answer to the question and shares a life lesson she learned while doing.*

**Angela LV**'s motivation to choose QR mainly stemmed from the richness of the data this type of research yields. As I have gathered more experience through studying, reading, and conducting QR, I have found that my capacity to think of a particular issue has expanded. I came to realize that a particular research tradition trains a researcher to think in certain ways. I may have not realized this when I chose a qual approach to research years ago. But now I see how that choice has impacted my life in ways that reach beyond my research work. As I have strived to understand and respect the perspectives of my participants, I have developed more tolerance and compassion for others. I am sure that these values have been greatly impacted by the choice of a research approach, together with the theories that have guided my studies.

CONCLUSION

Individuals choose to use QR/QM for their dissertation research for a variety of reasons, both personal and professional. As students, they have learned about the importance of their question related to their methodological choices. What struck me as I read the letters was how seldom I read: "It just felt like me." It may 'feel right' to many of the correspondents, but their thinking/reasoning means their senses have been influenced by the power of their educations. Regardless of where and when these correspondents learned about QR, they know from the beginnings of their experience that it is a credible and appropriate methodological approach for many of their questions. Their expectations for and experiences with QR are more sophisticated and in depth than the opportunities available to many research students during the last decades of the twentieth century. The learning and teaching that is going on now, "out there", is making a tremendous and valuable difference in the quality of research imagined and undertaken. Twenty-first century correspondents make excellent colleagues in learning because of the level of specificity and insight they share. **Crystal**'s letter below, with my title and italicized headings, provides one sense of cohesion to the experience of using qualitative research for the doctoral dissertation.

*"My Brother, My Self"* – Crystal Laura (*my title and subheadings*)

*Selecting our Topic…*

I spent the first three years of my doctoral experience dancing around my plans for dissertation research. The trouble wasn't that I could not identify what I wanted to know—I could. It wasn't that I did not understand how to go about doing the qualitative work to find out—I did. The real problem was that the meanings and perspectives that I was invested in capturing and relaying belonged to my own teen-aged brother.

*…for Purposes both Personal and Professional,*

Educators (and many others) have called my brother "bad" more than a few times. He was about five or six when he learned that he was "different"; at ten he was a "problem child"; at fifteen he was "disabled." Beyond that point, "dropout" seemed to him to be a natural progression. When he began flirting with the possibility of dropping out of high school altogether, I drew upon my identities and resources as a sister, a teacher, a student, and a scholar to defend my brother, to talk back to this nasty everyday discourse around him and so many other youth, to try my best to help him stay, excel, and be emotionally and spiritually well in school. The dissertation was one of many efforts to do all of this.

I wanted to study the plight facing adolescent black males in our public schools through the eyes of my little brother and a few of the people who love him dearly. The family was on board; some of my colleagues and professors at the university, not so much.

*while those Purposes and our Passion Compel us…*

Don't even get me started on the dilemmas and ethics of navigating and revealing our familial relationship. Is this research or therapy or investigative journalism? Whatever may be said for the case against studying so close to home, I believed then as I do now that a reconstructed account of how a "troublesome" child sees himself and the ways in which he and his family members reciprocally touch one another's lives would change the way that we think about under-education. This account would be an important counter-story to the written record. My brother's story would add to this canon, but it could also offer a unique opportunity to learn from a better-off black suburban family that we should care and worry about, but that we might not otherwise look to for insights on school-leaving experiences.

*…beyond Ourselves -*   More than anything, I hoped the process and product of my dissertation research might do something positive for my people; maybe help the family speak more intentionally, more often, and with greater insight; maybe nudge us to stop self-flagellating for my brother's educational trajectory; maybe hook us up with other folks who have experienced distress and failure in schools for support and perspective; maybe enable us to create happier and healthier places for us (and others) to learn and dwell. It was this deep investment in better understanding why leaving school made sense to him, what was going on with him in that moment, how he had come to that point, and where the places of conflict and change might have been that ultimately took the cake.

*- toward Professional Support and Encouragement,*   Knowing that the academic arena can be tough, I sought out and found several smart people within my institution and one outsider who really *got* what I was trying to do. In fact, they helped me see what I initially could not—that there was something new and exciting and significant about the thinking behind my work. My mentors pushed me to own it—to claim and defend my methodology and methods to a skeptical audience. So, I coined the phrase "intimate inquiry" and published *Home/work: Engaging the Methodological Challenges to and Possibilities of Intimate Inquiry* (Laura, 2010), an article that spells some of the ways that we can (and should) reframe what counts as educational research.

*enabling us to Succeed.* My advice to doc students, Judy, is quite simple: *keep it real* – with yourself and others. "Turn toward rather than away from the phenomenon of interest" – in my chair Bill Ayers' words – whatever it is that genuinely moves, enthralls, engages, enrages, and perplexes you. Open yourself to criticism by being honest and straightforward about how you are situated in the work. Say more about what brings you to the page, not less. Write into the tensions and contradictions inherent to all research, but especially your own. Lastly, trust the process and the good people whom you *must* surround yourself with. Onward, Crystal

> *As I hope you are beginning to appreciate, there is no way I could "quantiify" Crystal's letter to get at her and her correspondent colleagues' learning, thinking, and passion. Even if the letters are a synthesis reflection, it is in the telling, not the summary, that we connect to their learning, thinking, and doing, enabling us to think more deeply about who we are, what we choose to do, and why.*

*Table 4. Numbers vs. Rich Description: Why did you choose QR?*

|  | *Quantitative* | *Qualitative* |
|---|---|---|
| Word Count | 163 | 3247 |
| Pages | 1 | 7 |

# THE QUALITATIVE DISSERTATION

**Rich**'s dissertation is "traditional" if you consider three research manuscripts plus an introduction and conclusion traditional. I purposely tried to write a dissertation that could work as individual publications but also tell a cohesive narrative.

This was one area where I didn't have a lot of control. My advisor strongly recommended that I write my dissertation in this format. Listening to him, and now on the other side of my dissertation, I see the wisdom of this approach, as I have papers that can be (relatively) easily translated into journal format. To be very honest, I was willing to cede control of the format of the dissertation in order to ultimately control the content and the methods used to complete the research.

## INTRODUCTION

The final appearance of a qualitative thesis or dissertation has been the focus of some question and controversy for thirty years. One member of my committee, for example, thought concluding with hypotheses was "weird!" Although students early in their research careers might focus on the number of chapters and whose "voice" the document is written in, after engaging in the QR process, their attention to and concerns about "appearance" change.

### QUESTION SIX: WHAT DOES THE FINAL FORM OF YOUR DISSERTATION LOOK LIKE?

Table 5 below offers the chapter count and "description" of those correspondents who attended to this question. Yet, as **Rich** noted above, his five chapters might not be the same as yours. As with Part Two, use the table as either a synthesis of or an introduction to correspondents' decision making.

Following the table, you will notice that the correspondents provide what may appear as a litany of detail. However, there are more issues here than the obvious ones. Chances are, you may also find an experience that either mirrors or predicts your own thinking and doing.

*Table 5. Thesis Appearance, by number of chapters, appearance, locus of decision*

| # of Chapters | n | Appearance | n | Locus of Decision | n |
|---|---|---|---|---|---|
| 9 | 1 | "traditional" | 18 | requirements | 5 |
| 8 | 1 | > 6 chapters | 2 | my choice | 5 |
| 6 | 4 | novel aspects | 2 | my committee and me | 4 |
| 5 | 2 | traditional "if…" | 2 | my chair/advisor | 3 |
| 4 | 1 | - | - | my chair/advisor and me | 2 |
| - | - | - | - | my committee | 1 |
| Non report | 17 | Non report | 2 | Non report | 6 |
| Totals | 26 | - | 26 | - | 26 |

*Note.* N = 26 correspondents described specifics for this question.

**Roxanne**'s *format* was my department/major professor's choice for structure. I had originally wanted to have some case studies to give more information on individuals in my study, but my major professor thought I already had way too much information. She recommended saving them for a later publication. I had seven chapters.

**Jim O**'s dissertation was fairly traditional with the addition of one chapter for the participants' life stories. The chapters were: (1) Introduction, (2) Literature Review, (3) Methodology, (4) Life Stories, (5) Results, and (6) Conclusions.

**Jim B**'s format is fairly traditional, although I divided the findings into two chapters for better organization. I have a basic six chapter document: (1) Problem; (2) Literature Review; (3) Methodology; (4) Findings I; (5) Findings II; (6) Implications. The format decision was mine.

**Joan**'s format is the traditional six chapters, the choice of both me and my committee.

The final form for **Carita**'s dissertation is traditional; I am happy with the final outcome of the student stories, the research process, and the structure. **Mary** hopes my traditional dissertation has the feel of a story. I tried not to limit the LR to one chapter, but included it in several chapters. I also made full use of the first person researcher statement section. The format was a committee decision/requirement, *which is true for* **Sandy** *as well, but* I did have plenty of freedom in writing up the findings and discussion sections.

**Amanda**'s *thesis* has four chapters and is in some ways a dual (methodologically and in terms of content) dissertation. The number of chapters was at the discretion of my chair.

**Anabella** has a traditional QS where the results were presented in the form of data claims in response to analytic questions posed from the research questions of the study. These data claims summarized the common threads found in the data.

**Nancy**'s *thesis structure was also traditional.* This was my choice and the committee's. I think I needed to stick as close to a traditional format as possible. Had I come in with another form, I think it would have been an even harder sell to the committee.

The final form of **Lisa W**'s thesis is pretty traditional, although chapter four is a summary of the group sessions I attended, recorded and coded. I included a large bar chart to highlight the total topic utterances for each session, which was a joint decision between me and my chair. We had ongoing discussions of what a "traditional" dissertation would look like, and how I should make some changes to highlight the work I had done and give rich evidence of what had occurred in my research.

*For* **Francesca**, the traditional format is a department requirement no matter what the methodology. *The same holds true for* **Donna:** Although I would have liked more freedom to have written my thesis as a conversation, a novel of sorts, the graduate college and the department required the traditional way of writing up the study; there was even a template. **Ellie** chose to be traditional, and my committee agreed.

**Katherine** *had to work and rework her table of contents and format of her thesis. She makes explicit the dance of ownership and need to honor one's "creative spirit" while working with others to produce a final product satisfactory to all.*

I was encouraged to be "creative" but keep a semblance of recognizable components so as not to freak readers out too badly! While my dissertation doesn't follow the traditional 5 chapter format, it does have a balanced "skeleton" that is recognizable to traditionalists. Within the proposed structure, below, I was able to infuse my creative spirit.

Prologue

Chapter I: Introduction
Chapter II: Student Identities Matter
Chapter III: Organizational Culture Matters
Chapter IV: Methodological and Theoretical Foci
Chapter V: A Confluence of Forces
Chapter VI: The Materialization of a School Culture
Chapter VII: A Polyvocal Account of the Enactment and Negotiation of School Culture
Chapter VIII: Theory-building, Implications, and Future Research
Epilogue

As I stated in a follow-up email, the *university* made me do some reformatting. They would not allow a "prologue" but would allow an "introduction." Since I couldn't have a prologue, I got rid of the free-standing epilogue; I integrated it into chapter 8. ☹ Oh, well, that's bureaucracy for you! I made it work! My description of the content of the original prologue and epilogue remained the same.

> Introduction: What is Past is Prologue
> Chapter I: Overview
> Chapters II–VIII: as above

The Prologue shows how in my case, "what is past is prologue." I use a montage of scenes to show how my life experiences have influenced my epistemology as well as my passions and interests. It is my way of "positioning the author" so that the reader is aware of who I am and what I am about before I share the study. It is very personal. I feel completely naked, and that is risky to me. I feel that I may be rejected for my transparency, but that it is only fair that I am that open. After all, those I studied were completely up front with me and are letting me tell their story for all to read.

The Epilogue is my chance to react to the data on a more personal level. I had made a decision to do an interpretive study that examined culture rather than take a critical stance. It was extremely important to take the stance of fellow stakeholder. In order to gain entrée and develop trust, I knew a more descriptive study was in order – not a critical one. I was not comfortable marching in to a research setting and playing the role of critical investigator. I genuinely just wanted to find out what was going on in this particular environment, how it was different from the generic school that the girls would otherwise attend.

I use the Epilogue to explore some of the issues that troubled me as a feminist researcher who fell in love with a community of people. In fact, the original title of my dissertation was "Facilitating Social Justice in a Single-sex Public School…" I changed the title to "Troubling Social Justice in a Single-sex Public School…" after writing the Prologue. I felt that this title better reflected the ironies of the situation and better problematized the implications of the data without criticizing the people that were acting on the best interests of the girls at the school. It is/was a precarious balance! Katherine

*Speaking of titles, what follows is another original letter specifically addressing this topic.*

### Of Titles and Tribulations – **Kandace** Knudson

With my consent, my dissertation leads a life of its own. With my support, it left the nest upon filing it officially with the appropriately empowered officers of the university, and from there, it sailed off to a cyber and print world whose boundaries I can't even fathom. But I was prepared for this journey and christened my dissertation to ensure as best I could that its life would help and not hinder my progress through an ambling career trajectory: I gave it a careful title.

Not always is the life of a thesis or dissertation title a helpful one. These capstone academic projects carry the weight and significance of a tremendous amount of studious stewing, producing, and learning; they stand as testaments to our achievements. As qualitative researchers, we dig through our data neck-deep and shape our analyses into documents that represent our best research as academics. We expect them to represent to others the knowledge we have produced. If we are not careful, however, they can be twisted or misinterpreted in ways we did not intend, ways that could be detrimental to our lives as academics. Our dissertations represent us, speak for the whole of us, as we find our way into the professional world as academics; if we are not careful, their titles can deliver a judgment of our abilities, knowledge and even humanity before we have an opportunity to prove otherwise.

Dissertation and thesis titles will appear where we least expect them: like a siren on the front page of our transcripts, on some job applications, in biographies we submit with grants or papers, on curriculum vitae. *Consider your dissertation's title as your calling card* until you are well established in your career and have created other masterpieces that represent your work more effectively than your dissertation.

We critical theorists cling to and wear like a badge of honor the complicated and catchy titles that reveal our wit and the complexity of the topics we study. However, beware that your dissertation may "out" you in ways you cannot imagine. Because qualitative researchers often wrestle with projects that delve into the inner workings of human relationships, they often address sensitive topics that by their nature ruffle the feathers of conservative souls that may hold important positions of power or influence over your career trajectory.

When submitting copies of transcripts for job applications, I noticed that the very first page of the transcript from the college where I earned my master's degrees boldly listed the titles of my completed theses. Not a big deal, right? These are projects that demonstrated the hard work I had completed, testaments to my achievement in the study of literature, critical theory, and pedagogy. One thesis examined the work of a transcendental American poet in the context of contemporary theory. Another included that same poet's work in a proposed application of a contemporary pedagogical theory. The titles of my master's theses seemed very appropriate at the time:

"America's Outlaw Bard: Clearly, Quite Sincerely Queer."

"The Pedagogy of Whitman: Queering the Curriculum."

I am very proud of these examples of my work at that stage in my career. I stand by the analyses, curricular approaches, and conclusions offered in them. At that time, I was interested in the ways that queer theory could and should be used in order to promote a more inclusive curriculum at the undergraduate level. However, after a few failed attempts at academic jobs where it was suggested to me privately that my "leanings" might have had something to do with my rejections, I realized that I wanted to be able to determine the conditions under which I released the details of that work.

Because I put these titles on my theses, they now live a life of their own. I have lost control of how I present my career achievements academically. When I submit a job application packet for an administrative position this week, I will hold my breath and hope for the best.

I have heard that I might be able to appeal to the university and change my titles, but now I have my dissertation and its work to represent me. Its title is staid and true, representative of the academic content of the work it describes: "Community College Freshman Composition Instructors' Choices of Readings: The Importance of Context." Some might argue I have sold out to conservative interests who prefer that academics be tame or in the closet. I argue that it pays to have as much control over one's history and one's career trajectory as possible. I would much rather spend my time and energy researching important topics from a critical theoretical perspective than defending myself against hollow attacks from those who little understand the kind of work we do. If I were to present myself to a progressive committee, I can easily emphasize the content and titles that would appeal to such an audience.

Giving my dissertation a boring title may seem like a cop out, but this is my journey, and I want to hold the compass. Kandace

*Knowing* Katherine's *thesis "has 8 chapters" would not inform you of the thinking behind the structure. Both contributions, above, make it clear that there is more to naming our work than we might be aware of/fully understand while we are in the midst of learning. While summative data has its place and value, the illuminated thinking and doing – and redoing – of recent Ph.D. and Ed.Ds. provides the tools learners need as they build their confidence and competence.*

The one "novel" aspect of **Cindy**'s dissertation is the inclusion of 20 color photos, which appear as the final appendix. These photos help to tell the story of the Vietnamese community college. When I asked my committee if it was acceptable to include these, everyone was very enthusiastic. They said, "I've never heard of this before, but why not?" University protocol did not have a written rule for photo inclusion, so I moved forward with my idea after receiving written approval from my advisor and then the dean.

The presentation of data was probably the most interesting section of the dissertation. **Ronn** wanted to capture the complexity of life in a doubled-up residence without a hyper-focus on 'shocking' or negative aspects. I decided to divide Chapter Four into two sections. The first section offered readers an opportunity to see "A Day in the Life" of each participant. I constructed this section through interviews and observations throughout the seven months of data collection. I then provided a draft of each vignette to the participants and asked for their feedback. For the most part they agreed that I had captured a 'typical' day in their lives; however, I also made changes based upon their recommendations. I hoped that this approach would allow readers to get a sense of who the participants were as well as affording an opportunity to peek into the apartments where they lived. This section also included a visual representation of each residence to illustrate how space was divided.

The second portion of the chapter organized data based upon risk and protective factors. I discussed how experiences and perceptions changed over time as well as drawing out themes. The two sections of the chapter worked together to provide a depth of understanding as to how residences function as well as change over time.

*I clustered the brief responses of* Tiffany, Kj, Isabelle, Amy, *and* Isabeau *below because although concise, I believe they hold several "ah hah" moments about teaching and learning that are worth considering?*

Traditional. My choice, *replied* **Tiffany**, **Kj**, *and* **Isabelle**, *who added* simply because I had no idea I could do otherwise.

Traditional, **Amy** *thinks*, although at times it feels like it is trying to fit a square peg into a round hole. I think it is because the formats for papers I have done in classes have been traditional; it is all I've been exposed to. **Isabeau** thinks it will be very traditional. I would love to be more creative, but I just don't have the energy to do that.

**Angela LV**'s dissertation had a rather traditional format. My advisor played a major role in helping me decide the form. Her own work aligns with more traditional forms of QR.

**Angela F** *is one of more than several correspondents who, like* Katherine *more specifically above, related her understanding of her project to her view of it and the world.*

At first **Angela F** would say it was just that it fit with my way of looking at the world but in thinking about it now I realize that it was about the location of responsibility in qualitative research. I wanted the responsibility to own my decisions and believe that to do less is to diminish my own power and if I do that, it is inevitable that I will not be able to acknowledge the power of others. That qualitative research, at least interpretive qualitative research, requires one to acknowledge their own place and decisions in creating the world around them, is to me at the very core of being responsible to the world.

CONCLUSION

At first glance and read through, one might be tempted to think that Table 5 provided the information that so many individual correspondents seem to repeat, i.e., The form of my dissertation is "traditional... traditional... traditional."

However, it is difficult to find any two correspondents who have used exactly the same thesis format for the same reasons. Many have had some input into their sense of its "whole". I wonder what your thesis will look like when it finishes with you?

*Table 6. Numbers vs. Rich Description: What does your thesis look like?*

|  | *Quantitative* | *Qualitative* |
| --- | --- | --- |
| Word Count | 65 | 3170 |
| Pages | 1 | 8 |

### ESTABLISHING A CONTEXT: CONCLUSION

The environment for and context of qualitative research learning and doing has greatly changed. Regardless of a qual or quant "bent", twenty-first century learners are gaining a large repertoire of ideas and skills. They come from a great variety of backgrounds. They are not limited to one tradition or another. The repercussions of their capacity to raise questions and to set forth and answer them, conscious of and selective among paradigms, can only be positive. Perhaps **Rich** says it best?

Ideally, we would all be bilingual – we would vacillate between qualitative and quantitative methods per the questions we want to ask. My dissertation was designed in this vein because I wanted to find a job in a business program. I am not *fluent* in both languages, but I wanted to show that I understood that different questions require different methods and approaches, and that while I favor qualitative methods, I can speak the language of quantitative methods as well. It is a powerful package if you can pull it off.

# DECISIONS, DECISIONS, DECISIONS

**Cindy:** In QR, the world is the lab, with few to no boundaries. This fact offers endless possibilities but also creates a host of decisions that a quant researcher would not have to make; it creates an overwhelming environment of constant choices; it can cause a lot of stress.

## INTRODUCTION

The purpose of Section Two is to explore issues and obstacles as the correspondents experienced them, from the beginning of the process introduced in parts one and two of Section One, through the end, which was foreshadowed in the descriptions offered in part three of that section. Like Section One, this section is also divided into three parts, allowing you to focus more easily on the portion of material immediately important to you.

There are no tables in this section. What you will find, however, are some longer portions of letters in several different formats, including a "split" letter; abbreviated letters, which I titled with correspondents' approval to highlight their focus as I perceived it; letters in "interview" format, because it was by asking questions of the letter that I could bridge my understandings; and whole letters, as I received them. Because there is so much material in this section, I found that the pursuit of a singular way of putting it together caused the correspondents' individual insights to blur into a sameness leading to dullness in me as reader and thereby diminishing the distinct nature of their individual experiencing. Perhaps for this reason Section Two remains the longest section of the book. May I remind you, however, to read whatever of it matters to you at the moment and *not* to pursue the pages one after the next merely because they exist. Just because this text is a book does not mean you have to take it literally – excavate it, spoon into it, DIVE IN wherever you wish – and of course, muse over what you discover!

The organization and placement of the correspondents' contributions in this section is the result of some attempt to bring the continuity of their thinking across the research endeavor as well as emphasize the many ideas shared. There are places where I intentionally put the offerings of correspondents with similar names together, so that you would *not* confuse them or think "which Michele/Michelle was that again?" or "Is that Isabeau or Isabelle?" Because I also use headings in this section, I have been able in several places to end one topic with a correspondent's writing and begin the next topic continuing with that same correspondent's thought.

However, as is the way of letter writing, the correspondents sometimes stressed certain points, jumped to others and then returned to conclude. My job then, in the three parts to this section and throughout the book, has been to put a few arbitrary starting and stopping points to the reflections in order to provide some cohesion to the topics shared. I admit to having found it a daunting task.

# BEGINNINGS

**Cassandra**: Soon after I was assigned a chair for my committee and met with her, I began to realize that a dissertation is more than telling a story in some loosely coupled fashion; it is a scientific approach to answering an important question that supposedly helps increase the body of knowledge on a particular subject matter.

## INTRODUCTION

To experienced qualitative researchers, the descriptions of where the correspondents learned about QR, why they have chosen it, and what their final thesis documents looked like, make clear some of the changes in the status of QR relative to IHEs during the last thirty years. More and more individuals are learning about QR at more and more universities and colleges, not only in the United States but around the world, not only at the doctoral level, but at the master's and undergraduate levels as well. Novice researchers are learning among experienced professors, many of whom choose QR for their own research, many of whom have contributed to our understandings of QR. Theses, which had an almost uniform, graduate 'requirement' appearance to them, range in numbers of chapters and 'voice', with the additional of student-topic-advisor inputs. Clearly the 21st century has much to commend it!

It is the case, however, that many of the same issues facing learners in the last decades of the 20th century related to learning about and doing QR remain, likely because they are a part of the learning process. Part One describes the issues confronting learners today at the beginnings of the process. The correspondents and I believe that knowledge about what can happen or might happen – and in many cases, what DID happen – will enable you better to prepare and perhaps avoid some of the difficulties doing QR presents. I begin with several general reflections and then turn to specific topics that tend to arise early in the research learning by doing process.

**Tiffany**: First off, it's HARD!! While it is much more interesting than quant research, I finds it much, MUCH harder. I did not expect that. I think I must have initially assumed it would be easier since I wouldn't have to worry about all those statistical measures. However, QR is so much more complicated in so many ways.

The questions raised by **Rich**'s work primarily involved the population. The most formidable of these concerned my ability to faithfully re-create my participants' responses. Interviews often took place in garages while equipment was running, outside in fields, or in noisy dairy operations. These instances prevented the use of a recording device, so I had to practice a style of taking notes that would allow me to re-create the content of our interview once returning to my office; part of this style was to also take time to write quotes when possible. I do not try to "remember" quotes. What I often did – since my participants were located up to 2 hours away from my office – was to find a local coffee shop and start writing as soon as the interview was complete. I became very effective at this process, though I was definitely questioned about it by my committee at my defense. Ultimately it is a solo practice without much evidence, so be prepared for questioning.

When the noise and location would have allowed me to record interviews, I often did not record because the service station owners asked me not to out of fear of retribution. This too was brought up at my defense; if I made a mistake in this area in writing my dissertation, it was to leave out all of the details about these methodological questions in the manuscript itself (it was already running quite long). My committee didn't hold me up or suggest major revisions due to my omissions, but I could have saved myself a line of questioning by proactively addressing these issues.

The major issue **Amanda** faced was being the first researcher known to complete a study using the meta-interpretation method. It was time intensive and required much reflection and journaling in addition to maintaining an audit trail.

The only issue for **Julie** has been internal. I have had a lot of work to do mentally to psych myself up for the task.

## HONORING INTERESTS

As **Michele,** *who earned a DMA in 2010,* began the doctoral program, my expectation was that I would learn to be a better practitioner. I did not understand how much research would be involved in my coursework and was surprised to find that a person could receive a doctorate in music education without participating in private lessons or an ensemble. This fact really troubled me, so I made it a point to audition for the choir and continued to study private voice, allowing me to work on my personal musicianship as well as my research skills.

**Corey** was not well versed in narrative analyses. I was a numbers guy. I had a strong background in mathematics, but not in English. I knew from the get go that I was going to have my work cut out for me. However, my strong Type-A personality was always looking for a challenge, and this was certainly going to be one.

It was quite the struggle at first. It took a couple of classes for me to really begin to understand the concept behind QR. Fortunately, to keep me on the quant side, my program required 2 quarters of statistics.

## JUSTIFYING QR

Many people at the university level are skeptical of QR and don't feel it has the "rigor" of quant research, so **Kj** battled stereotypes from some professors and students.

Individuals outside the realm of **Anabella**'s doctoral program would ask what I wanted to study or what I was studying through my dissertation. I would tell them that it was a qual study on undergraduate students' experiences of learning research. They would respond in a way that made me feel like I needed to justify my study in significant ways for them to believe/consider that I was doing worthwhile research. I can't say at this point if this was due to the topic itself or the research approach, but the feeling was there.

**Ginny** was concerned with whether or not my study would be considered credible, I guess, since I had no statistics or numbers that could provide "definite proof" of what I discovered. I was afraid that people would not take my work seriously if I didn't have quantitative results.

I also found that conducting and writing a QS to be more involved than I initially thought. I had imagined I would ask questions and a conversation would ensue with the participant that would shed light upon my theories. I would write about it and that would be all. I soon discovered that a whole lot more time and effort went in to preparing and justifying what I wanted to study, and it took a very long time to get to that point.

**Nancy** was told time and again that my study findings would not be generalizable. I acknowledged this and let faculty know I understood their concern. To bolster my study, I found a great deal of research that supported the methodology. I did a critical collective case study with a purposeful sample. I chose classic sources for my methodology section that would convince my readers of its legitimacy.

I did feel that I needed to provide additional evidence to show that my methods were legitimate. I almost changed my research design to a quant study because I was afraid I wouldn't be able to complete my dissertation if I didn't. My committee chair nixed the idea and helped me push through. But there were a lot of tears throughout the process. All in all, my QS was much harder, yet much more rewarding, than my quant master's study.

## LITERATURE REVIEW

If **Aaron** would have done anything sooner it would have been starting my LR. I had a general idea of what I wanted to study coming into school, a burning question if you will. However, I was not able to shape that question because I didn't know what was known or, in my case, *not* known in the field, until I spent the time to do a thorough LR. I discovered the gap in the literature, which led to the formation of my question, which led to my design. So if I had it to do over again, I would be serious about the LR and the cataloguing of resources around it on day one. I was so concerned about learning about methods that I put myself in a hole that took a semester to dig out of, lengthening my time to completion.

**Jim B** would recommend keeping a short one to two phrase summary of your research question close by. I found this strategy very helpful for keeping me on track with my research. It is easy to get distracted by interesting books, journal articles, and other people's (finished) dissertations when you are reviewing literature for your own work. I think this temptation to get off track can be even stronger for QR because your observations and your participants' stories likely include much more information in addition to the specific data you are collecting. While your interests in your topic may be broad, your dissertation question is typically narrow; returning to my question periodically was a helpful check to be sure I was not veering off on a tangent.

**Michele** really struggled with completing the LR. My topic was music teacher identity; it took me a long time to understand that. At first, I looked at student and beginning teacher lit, and music education student lit. Then, I looked at the socialization lit. Many of the participants discussed issues with classroom management, so I read that literature. It took me a very long time to discover which articles, books, and dissertations were relevant to my study and which were just "interesting." At one point, I grew quite frustrated because I felt I had read many unnecessary studies. In retrospect, however, I think it was important for me to do that.

**Liz** suggests not inserting a 60 page LR into your proposal or dissertation. Feedback from a peer and my advisor when I did this was that my review, while good, was far broader than the scope of my work and wasn't clearly aligned to my conceptual framework. The data can pull you in a million directions (and interesting ones, to boot!), but for the immediate present, focusing on the research questions you set out to answer is critical if you ever want to complete the dissertation.

## ORGANIZATION

**Michele** was immediately challenged by my lack of organization. I was studying six beginning teachers; each taught at a different school in different areas of the city. I gathered information in many ways including observations, interviews, emails, phone calls, and artifacts; initially, I found it impossible to keep track of all that information. I tucked scraps of papers in my daily planner, scribbled notes on napkins while speaking with participants on the phone, and even found myself writing down notes while driving down the road. I do not recommend this last technique!

Because there are so many elements involved in a QRD, **Michelle** asserts you must be organized. I am doing a case study with four teachers. For each I need to observe two classes four times and conduct three interviews; I need one interview with each teacher's administrator, as well as with three of his/her students. The teachers' schedules and mine have to fit together, requiring me to make a chart and organize the times. I then needed to keep track of when I accomplished each of the above tasks. Without organization, it could be very confusing. Charts helped me a lot.

## FACULTY RESOURCES

**ANON** It is only retrospectively that I am able to realize how many challenges I did face upon deciding to use QR for my thesis. Although my advisor had done some QR, I came to realize s/he was more of a quant researcher who did some qual research. At my institution quant research is much more common. I had a hard time finding people with whom I could talk through methods and resource issues. I did a lot of searching on my own. I did check in with 3 other students who had recently completed QDs. While somewhat helpful, it was not as if I were having in-depth conversations with my chair or committee members about QM or the details of my project.

The way my advisor ran his/her committees was to be the primary contact; all conversations went through him/her, which meant I was not supposed to contact the committee's qual "expert" directly. When I was in my defense this individual brought up some methodological questions he/she had, leading to a lot of additional work and revising. Knowing how your advisor operates thesis committees is vital to your dissertation process and progress.

**ANON** When our school got a new dean a couple of years ago, support for QR dwindled. Many of the qual-friendly faculty members have retired or gone elsewhere. Our program seemed like it was fairly balanced when I applied, but once I started classes, I found this was not true. The online program overview now states that doctoral students will be able to identify and ask questions that can be answered using quantitative methods.


## DEVELOPING QUESTIONS

For **Isabelle** the research questions were the biggest issue. It took a while to develop them. Without well-defined questions my project might be crippled. I spent a lot of time rewording them until I was satisfied. From there, the choice of methodology became evident. Developing a questionnaire to establish learners' stereotypes also proved to be tricky. Right away I had to confront my own subjectivity:

> I started to realize that most of the questions could pose problems because they were stereotyping or essentializing the object of study…. I began to think that I would expose my participants to stereotypes and assumptions that they may not even be familiar with…. Therefore, I decided to change my approach and follow a more qualitative avenue to elicit … data. (p. 82)

> I went through multiple versions of the questionnaire, wanting to avoid my own preconceived ideas of American stereotypes of French people. I piloted and piloted and …, finally reaching a consensus. I chose to use open-ended questions.

## VOICE

**Angela F**'s dissertation journey was about finding my own voice. As a woman, first generation college student from a working class background, I actually sometimes struggled with some of the qual principles of giving voice to others. I was in a process of expressing my voice and my experience; I struggled to find a balance with this and to come to the notion of speaking "with not for" and being transparent in my own voice and interpretation.

**Vic** recently finished my QD and found the adventure to be combinations of clarity and confusion, immersion and detachment, excitement and frustration. In the end, though, I believe I found my voice; I was able to portray the findings through a depth of understanding that only QI lends itsef to.

## SETTING LIMITS

One of **Cindy**'s biggest obstacles was setting limits. I started meeting with my Qual 1 and 2 professor, Dr. Althof. The first time, I told him I wanted to do 11 or 12 case studies. He replied that I needed to limit myself to three or four that represented all 12. He made several suggestions for limiting the scope of the study. I had developed and nurtured my informant and had access to all but one of the 12 existing community colleges in Viet Nam. He thought it was too much and would result in so much data that I would not be able to complete it in the time I had available. I continued to be adamant with my plan. I went into it knowing that my month of visits would be physically, emotionally and intellectually exhausting.

## SELECTING A SITE

Be aware of the setting you select for data collection. **Brighid** was initially interested in collecting data at a historically Black college or university (HBCU). However, HBCUs have had a long negative history with researchers conducting inappropriate research on their campuses. Prior to beginning my dissertation research I had worked a lot with HBCUs and HBCU students and was well trained in conducting culturally sensitive and appropriate research. Nonetheless, I was viewed as an outsider because I did not attend an HBCU. I had to undergo a full IRB review at these institutions although my home institution found my study exempt from a full review.

## INSTITUTIONAL REVIEW BOARD (IRB)

**Tom** needed to convince the IRB that my research would be suitable and safe for my participants. At the time, a number of tenured professors who were quant in outlook sat on the IRB; I had to be creative in the draft of my proposal in regard to vocabulary. My dissertation chair was well versed in both methodologies and able to help me use synonyms in my proposal that would help it get through the board. Luckily, it did on one try. Some of my colleagues had issues of getting their proposals accepted, but eventually all did get through this first hurdle.

**Megan** submitted an initial application to the IRB to the institution where I would receive the degree. My committee had me submit the proposal for exempt status, as I would be conducting interviews and utilizing information from reflection papers written by students about their incidents two years earlier. I submitted the application in mid April.

On April 29th, I was advised that it did not meet exempt status … rather it should be resubmitted as an expedited application. I then submitted two expedited applications – one to each institution – on April 30th.

On May 7th, I was advised by the institution where I would be receiving the degree that the application needed to be resubmitted as a full application. Additionally, the email stated:

> Also, it has been suggested that you attend the meeting so you can be available to provide any guidance during the discussion. The next Full Committee meeting is scheduled for June 11.

When I called the IRB office to inquire if my advisor needed to also be present and what I could expect at the full meeting, I was informed, "It would behoove you to have your advisor there with you"… and "I don't know what to tell you to expect as the board has never asked for a primary investigator to attend the full meeting before."

On May 18th, the application was accepted as expedited by the institution where the study would take place, which was also forwarded onto the full IRB committee.

On June 11th, my advisor and I attended the full IRB meeting. Among many questions I was asked, the question that has stuck and will ever remain in my memory was, "And why do you think that these students would agree to talk to you about what happened to them two years ago?" It had never occurred to me that they wouldn't … but that question put a lot of doubt into my mind as to whether or not I had chosen to pursue the "right" topic… and whether or not a qualitative dissertation was achievable. It might have been easier to just do a quantitative study.

On July 3rd, the committee approved the proposal BUT couldn't release the Assurance Letter of Approval because my advisor needed to complete the IRB tutorial as she showed in their records as someone who was, according to the email, "not current with our Human Subjects Tutorial or their training will be expiring shortly."

Between April and July, it should also be noted that there were many email and phone calls asking for more clarification; more examples; more questions; more concerns.

Finally, on August 25th, I received an email stating, "Your Assurance Letter of Approval and IRB stamped consent form is being sent to you by way of U.S. Mail. Good luck with your study." Approval came over 4 months after the first proposal was submitted.

Although the IRB process was long and arduous, causing many tears, frantic moments, and more work, it did end up being useful. It helped me clarify what I was doing and why. It reminded me I was tapping into a relatively unexplored area. It reminded me to keep ethical considerations in the forefront of all I did. I had been privy to very sensitive information in my past and current roles at a small private college, information I needed to protect. I believed the students' stories were important to share and would inform practice. And, despite some doubt and a little wavering, I was willing to go the distance to be allowed to voice their words. Finally, the IRB experience reminded me that whatever the timeline I had created for myself, it was inevitably subject to things outside of my control. I had to find peace with that and challenge my own thinking to focus on the final goal, not the temporary frustration.

**Ronn** chose to conduct a study of families forced to live together as a result of economic crises, i.e., doubled-up youth. The case study meant that I would be spending extensive time in four apartments where multiple families lived. My goal was to understand how this residential structure framed the educational experiences of adolescents.

The first major obstacle involved navigating IRB. It was concerned I might see or hear about illegal activity while observing and interviewing in South Central Los Angeles. After two months of working with IRB, I agreed to take a few steps to limit my exposure to illegal activity: (a) I would include a warning prior to conducting interviews that encouraged participants not to share illegal activity; (b) I would refine questions to limit comments about drug use and gang violence; (c) I would ask participants not expose me to illegal activity during observations; and, (d) I would code data in a way that would make it difficult to connect participants to illegal activity.

I then had to gain access to this subpopulation of homeless adolescents, which tends to be invisible. Also, adolescents in doubled-up residences (as well as other forms of residential instability) experience high levels of shame. Lack of visibility coupled with shame made access a challenge. I had been working with organizations supporting homeless youth and low-performing schools in Los Angeles for nearly two years. I had met one youth living in a doubled-up residence while participating in a previous study. His family agreed to participate and introduced me to another family in their complex. I then contacted two youth who participated in a mentoring program where I volunteered. My relationship with the youth prior to beginning the study allowed me to establish trust necessary to gain access to their homes. Had I not been involved in their communities I would not have been able to conduct this study.

**Monica** spent 4 unsuccessful months trying to get IRB approval at another institution to interview their students. Without knowing anyone there, it was impossible to gain entry.

## GAINING ENTRY

**Amy**'s biggest obstacle was gaining access to a site. I moved across the country for grad school, and while I attend an education school, few people in my program have ever been teachers and none had taught in the immediate area. My only option was to start emailing and calling principals. Most emails and phone calls were not returned. The principals who responded were not willing to let me observe in their schools – partially, I suspect, because I am interested in schools that have been labeled as "failing" under NCLB.

I finally found a school willing to give me access. Once I had the go-ahead from the superintendent, I was able to start contacting teachers. Again, I was doing this via email as the principal would not let me attend a staff meeting because they were gearing up for the state testing and did not have the time to spare. I finally found a teacher willing to talk with me. She passed along a few names of teachers she thought would be willing to work with me, and most of them were. I was able to conduct my study mostly the way I intended to from the start.

For **Debra,** the time spent speaking to an individual often is preceded by months of back-and-forth exchanges. My post-9/11 dissertation involved interviews with staff working in military child development centers. Clearly, the US military is extremely security-conscious. The individuals who helped me gain access to the child development centers could not have been more enthusiastic about my study, but gaining access took about nine months. (I would advise not sharing this bit of information with your quant pals unless you are prepared to be ridiculed about how "long" it is taking you to finish your dissertation.)

Gaining access also took on new meaning each time I visited, as I needed to first go through a scripted security procedure to enter a base. This involved parking my car, presenting my credentials to the security center staff, and posing for my temporary visitor badge photo, as well as allowing my car to be thoroughly searched by armed (but always polite!) military police. I have an embarrassing memory of the first time this occurred and not having any idea of how to release the hood of my car so my engine, etc, could be cleared as free from explosives. Fortunately, the young man who was conducting the search took pity on my clueless state and got in the front seat himself so he could find the magic hood-release lever.

Networks are vital to gaining access; **Brighid** did not know anyone at the possible sites where I wanted to collect data. I was not permitted to contact the people I thought would have connections to these institutions. After trying to gain access to a site for over a year, I ended up having to change sites. After 5 months without success I had to change my dissertation topic and write a new proposal.

SAMPLE

The first major choice **Jim O** had to make was who would be included in my sample. The responsibility of telling my participants' stories accurately and being able to understand their viewpoints was very important to me. As a gay man, I felt confident that I could relate, understand, and convey the life histories/stories of other gay, lesbian, and bisexual people. I was not sure I could do an adequate job of truly understanding a transgendered person's life experience given the fundamental difference between <u>sexual</u> and <u>gender</u> identity. After much discussion with my committee, we decided to exclude the transgender population.

In setting up **Tom**'s study, I sent out an initial survey to the entire alumnae of the school. The first returns were great, and then there was nothing. I was dumbfounded because I had included a prepaid return envelope to make it easy. I had to send out three follow up letters in order to elicit more responses. I was trying to throw out a wide net in the first part of my research in order to craft follow up questions for focus groups.

ADVICE: Be prepared to be frustrated and also be ready for a lack of response from the people you want in your study. The next step was to bring in alumnae for focus groups. Once again, I was naïve to think they would jump at this chance to catch up and discuss what had happened. I was hoping to have three focus groups but only had two successful ones take place.

All three groups were very reticent at the start, but then after a few warm-up questions the conversation flowed. ADVICE: Have a good recording device. My first focus group's recorder was okay, but then I borrowed a friend's digital voice recorder; it went very well for the second group. Keep in mind that you need to transcribe all these conversations; this is where the bulk of your time will be spent, if done well.

**Veronica** knew my participants would be [ones] who had taken my course. A main criterion for selection was that the participants had experienced the teaching process demonstrated and practiced in this course. I began the selection process eight months prior to my research, asking students to provide me with their email and phone number if they would be interested in participating in my research at a later time. While there was a purpose for this selection criterion, it did limit my sample considerably. I had a total of 60 people from which to draw; I hoped at least five would participate.

Eight months passed. I began the recruitment process as I had planned by calling or emailing those students who had shown interest, i.e., 15 of the 60 students. Of these 15, only 9 responded. Four who did respond were not in their student teaching phase or in a teaching position, leaving me with exactly five potential participants.... Later, one of my participants emailed me to opt out of the study, using the photo-elicitation process:

> "I picked a picture of the ocean because it is so immense, overwhelming. That is how I felt, overwhelmed, not just with your study, but [with] what I had to do to graduate ... [and with] my responsibilities as a TEACHER, as a BOYFRIEND, as a PET OWNER, all these different things that I needed to do and take care of."

I knew that without nurturing the relationships with my participants, I would have had no data. Furthermore, I didn't' realize until after my study how much I was asking of my potential participants. I hope to be more cognizant of the physical and mental demands of participating in research as I continue in my development as a researcher.

**Roxanne** had a gatekeeper for one group of participants, but the trouble was finding participants from the general population. **Kristan** had challenges finding high school students who were willing to participate for a long time, about ten months in some cases. I tried a few sites before finding the one that would work, which caused about a month delay in starting data collection. I realized I had to go where the stories were and where there were individuals willing to share them.

Because so many of the young women in the study had few adults on a consistent basis in their lives, I had to be mindful of how I developed relationships with them over the course of ten months of data collection. At one point in the study, I had a student who had been telling me for a month that things were going well in her life when actually, they weren't. When I finally found out that she was not being accurate, I wasn't sure what to do with the data. Did it still "count?" And if so, how? When I asked her about it, we were able to go through the accuracies and inaccuracies of her statements together. I think it was a learning experience for both of us. In the end, I feel like the final version of the study participant's life was real.

The careful and calculated selection of your research subjects is the key to validity and reliability. With almost 9,000 miles between St. Louis, Missouri, and Viet Nam, **Cindy** had many obstacles to finding reliable subjects. Developing relationships so that people trusted me was my first step. A few years before thesis work began, I started reading everything I could on Viet Nam as a society. When I found a book/article that offered insights, I went online, found out how to contact the author and sent an email. I shared my interest and asked a lot of "help me understand" questions and "Can you connect me with anyone from your research?" I was amazed at the results. Every scholar I contacted was helpful, offered more contacts than I had expected and shared as much as I was willing to take. I found Dr. Diane Oliver who had written a dissertation on the Vietnam community college model in 2002. When I emailed her, she immediately replied with a sharing attitude that could be summed up with this statement: I am so happy to know that someone else is interested in the topic.

**Sandy** chose to conduct a multiple case study, which involved identifying three institutions that were willing to participate. I contacted vice chancellors at each institution by email to explain my study and request their institutional participation. After meeting the selection criteria, I decided I would take the first three that agreed. I then had to identify 5–9 individuals at each institution to interview and had to coordinate their availability and mine. I wanted to visit each campus, so I made the choice to fly to three locations and stay two nights in each city. Scheduling this was a challenge, but I ended up traveling once a month for three consecutive months to collect my data.

**Michelle** moved to a new state with a new job; I contacted presidents of organizations already in place to help me find participants and gain entry.

*"The Sample from Sampling"* – **Annie** Jonas (*Annie's letter, my title*)

Dear Dr. Meloy: I appreciate that you are focusing on the QD process and would love to contribute. I would like to think my experiences may assist others on their dissertation journey. I am in the research phase of a QD. My proposal title, "*Practices of Experiential Teachers in Secondary Schools in an Age of Accountability*" may give you a sense of the focus and direction for my study. My proposal was approved in September 2010, and I have been gathering research in local public high schools since that time.

As I reflect on my research experience and the overall dissertation process to date, I think my greatest learning (and challenge) has been in experiencing, and responding to, the evolving nature of qualitative research. I was theoretically prepared for this through guidance from my professors, focused reading on this topic, graduate courses in research and a graduate pre-dissertation seminar. All of this preparation and support would suggest that I should not have been surprised by this "gray" process. However, to actually experience the need to toss out a definitive black and white framework and the accompanying loss of focus was a shock for me.

My accepted dissertation proposal outlined a process by which I would select 8–10 teachers to be the focus of my study. I proposed to find these teachers through reputational case sampling and ultimately select them for the study after focused observations in their classrooms. During the exhausting 2½ months of searching for names and observing in various classrooms across the county I began to lose momentum and enthusiasm for my topic. I experienced a sinking feeling that my research was never going to happen, that I would be stuck in this search process indefinitely. The original momentum I felt after the approval of my proposal was quickly waning. I felt a loss of direction and an uncomfortable sense of helplessness about the whole process. The time it was taking me to find teacher names, receive approval from respective teachers (and the appropriate administrative bodies), settle on observation times, and actually observe was extensive and exhausting. And then to realize that more often than not I was not uncovering strong examples of my phenomenon of interest left me feeling completely frustrated.

Just in time, I had a change of heart. One afternoon, after observing one truly exemplary (of the practice of interest) teacher, I sat in the back of his classroom after students had filed out. As I wrote in my journal about what I had just witnessed (and my personal reactions), I realized how much rich material this one class was offering me. I don't know how I missed seeing this originally, except that I had been completely focused on finding 8 to 10 teachers, rather than appreciating the few really excellent examples I had been able to uncover. Suddenly I had a vision of what direction this dissertation might take if I were willing to abandon my original proposal. A flash of light occurred when I realized that I could learn much more from an in-depth study of one or two teachers, rather than focusing on the larger number I had outlined in my proposal. Accompanying this excitement about a possible new direction was the unsettling recognition that I had perhaps wasted a lot of time figuring this out. The even greater dreaded recognition was that this new direction would require rethinking (and resubmitting) my proposal.

This story serves to highlight the unfolding process in research, particularly qualitative research. After recognizing that a more focused study (case study) would provide me with the data I was most interested in, I still had to sit with the uncomfortable realization that I would need to take two steps back in order to take one step forward. Once I released myself to take these steps backward, it was amazing how much momentum and enthusiasm for my topic returned. I ultimately submitted a revised proposal to my committee and restructured my data collection process to include student voices (via interviews). The inclusion of student interviews required that I resubmit IRB forms as well.

While it felt like a set-back while in the middle of the process, I clearly see now that I needed to walk through the confusion and lack of direction, in order to gain from it. I have a heightened sense of the phenomenon I am studying because of the challenges it required to get to where I am now. I have learned a lot along the way but this particular snapshot highlights what stands out to me as being the most challenging and rewarding to date. Sincerely, Annie 2.28.11

## JOURNALS

**Angela F** kept a journal throughout my whole doctoral process. It was a place where I documented the path to finding my specific research interest.

A writing notebook is an essential tool. When **Jim B** started writing the proposal, I bought a new notebook and kept all of my outlines, memos, sketches, and notes in it. I kept it in my backpack; whenever I had a question/insight, I would jot it down. Some entries were a phrase or two, others were several pages. There was no format or formality to it. I gave myself permission to write down ideas with no commitment to use them in the dissertation, giving me the freedom to explore angles and perspectives I was not sure would "fit" without feeling as though I had to think it through before writing, and allowing for the consideration and re-consideration necessary to qual work. The writing notebook was particularly helpful in sketching out my conceptual framework, figures, and tables as they evolved along with my dissertation study.

## CONCLUSION

*I choose to conclude part one with an extended description in interview format from* **Sarah**, *who writes*: A friend told me her doctoral degree experience had been "life changing and transformative." I was doubtful that at my age I was in for such an experience, but it happened.

*"Visual Imagery and the IRB"* – (*abridged, my title*) – Sarah Deaver
Nearing 60 years of age, I had actually given up on the idea of a doctoral degree, since there was no feasible program offered locally, and I am tied to the area because of my husband's practice. I finally opted instead for a costly kitchen remodel. Then Old Dominion University started a doctoral program. Through a series of fortunate coincidences, I was offered a full scholarship. I couldn't refuse, so embarked upon

the course of study and graduated at age 62 in 2009. So I now have both a beautiful new kitchen and a marvelous new diploma, and Judy, I loved it all, especially the dissertation.

1. *How did you learn about qualitative research?* For many years, I supervised art therapy master's degree students on their **quantitative** thesis projects. I had struggled to educate my IRB about art therapy research....

Then when attending the American Art Therapy Association conference in 1999, I went to a session called "The Sabbath Bride" (Allen, 1999). In that session, a preeminent art therapist showed slides of a large, complex painting she had created, and described her creative process as "research." Solid in my conviction that *real* research was always quantitative, I asked, "How is what you have presented *research?*" The answer given stumped and confused me, and led me to read about QR. I didn't come around to embracing it until some years later when a student chose to use interview methods to discover the role of artmaking in the lives of Holocaust survivors. The IRB informed me that the student's study was "not research." In my effort to convince the board that this QS was in fact research, I convinced myself.

2. *Why did you choose qualitative research for your dissertation?* I chose a qual approach because there was no published research about the use of visual journaling as a catalyst for reflection during master's degree students' clinical internships. In addition, my QR teacher was immeasurably (no pun intended) inspirational, supportive, and patient with me as I wrestled with the multiple fascinating assignments in her class. Throughout the semester I became more and more excited about the prospect of a QS.

*Tell me more about the assignment, Sarah?*

It had to do with my own visual journal that I employed throughout my doctoral work. I had analyzed my entries in relationship to various academic, personal, and professional activities throughout one semester. I remember being extremely anxious about it because I had included an example of a page from my journal. My professor loved the image; her endorsement of my work convinced me that I could pursue a QD – even one that included imagery. This professor later became my methodologist; she sent me your call for contributors.

3. *What issues/ obstacles/ choices did you face once you made your decision to use it?* The first challenge was having been essentially assigned a chair who didn't love my dissertation idea, or the idea of a QS. He asked, "But what will we have in the end?" I had been encouraged to seek this person as a chair, although not a good fit; I labored on. The dilemma was resolved when he told me he would not be available in the summer to review any of my work. I got permission to change chairs and found the perfect fit with a different, supportive, professor.

An additional challenge was both the hunch that my IRB would never approve using my own art therapy students as research participants and the realization that my study would be more credible if I did not. A colleague offered her students, which meant driving 9 hours each way, four times, over about 16 weeks. I grew to love my long weekends with the students and....

4. *What supports did you have?* I found strong support particularly from my chair and my methodologist, who was another outstanding QR expert. The program director, not so much; however, he was one of my committee members and was very pleased with my study. He is now chairing a QD committee – I believe we are making a convert of him!

5. *What methodological questions were raised by your work? How did you answer them?* My chair and I wrestled over how to think about one of my categories and finally were able to agree. My methodologist initially thought a lot of the material about my participants' general responses need not be included. However, since there is no published research about art therapy students' emotional responses to internships, she agreed to let me keep that material in.

6. *What does the final form of your dissertation look like?* My program determined the general format: it included the traditional five chapters and a sixth that was a journal manuscript ready for publication. Also included was a brief CV.

What made my dissertation different was the inclusion of images of journal pages, which I used in combination with quoted interview material to illustrate the patterns and themes that emerged through the data analysis. I was grateful that my committee recognized the value of including the images.

7. *Is there anything else you'd like to share or suggest?* Keeping a journal – whether written or one that combines artmaking and writing – is an essential aspect of the dissertation process. I maintained my visual journal throughout my studies. It helped me understand both the difficulty of finding time for this practice and the value of the journal as a process and a "place" in which to reflect upon and sort through experience.

The piece I share below is about 6" × 6" and contains magazine pictures, hand-made and printed papers, rusted hardware, and brass beads. The vertical image on top depicts a Chinese figure playing a flute, and behind that is a magazine photo of a receding stepped path. This is one of a series of several collages inviting the viewer to come inside and in some way walk through them.

My current employer is a medical school, and I have had to educate my biomedical IRB regarding qualitative research methodologies, including art-based research, interviewing techniques, and data analysis approaches. My primary IRB contact says that my art therapy research protocols are "challenging" for him and the reviewers but "very interesting."

# GETTING INTO IT

**Karen R:** It just so happens that the questions I asked sent me in the direction of QM!

## INTRODUCTION

Although I had originally scattered **Karen R**'s response across the six sections of this book, she sent me the following email related to the abridged "play with" file I had created for her letter. (In her case, I had used the focus questions to guide my selections and write the "interview".) "Judy: It looks/reads very well, and I can 'hear' my voice there much more clearly than I did in the last version (or at least how I remember it now) Karen, June 25, 2011." Because at the time of publication Karen R is still a doctoral student, I decided to use her writing as an exemplar of "getting into it".

1. Karen, *How did you learn about QR?* I have always been interested in methodology; my doctoral coursework had a decidedly methodological bent. Over three years, I became *particularly* interested in thinking about QMs and their potential in areas that up until now have been approached largely using quant methods.

I also had the true pleasure of taking a course my first semester on the theoretical underpinnings of research methodology. Although this course focused on both qual and quant methods, it was here I began to realize the limitations of quant research and potential of QM to fill many gaps left by researchers using quantitative techniques.

2. *Why did you choose it?* I came to graduate school with my dissertation topic already in mind; I had completed a master's degree in a different field and while there became interested in the question that ultimately became my focus. I was able to take advantage of my coursework, then, to learn a lot about different qual and quant approaches. The methodological approach I finally chose takes the issues in a new direction and will (hopefully) make much more of a contribution than if I used a quant approach.

3. *What issues/obstacles/choices did you face?* A number of people who do research in my area questioned [and continue to question] my methodological choices. I have found myself on the defensive on numerous occasions and have not yet come up with a good way to respond to critiques of my approach.

When I have conversations with these detractors, I end up more flustered than anything else. I think this speaks to the difficulty of choosing the non-dominant path in general – but it is frustrating nonetheless.

4. *What supports for it exist at your university?* I am lucky to have a wide variety of support systems. Of the four faculty members in my substantive sub-field, three are qual researchers; two are anthropologists by training. Our program requires students to take at least one QM course, but most students take many more than that. Courses focus on critical methodology, feminist methods, narrative analysis and discourse analysis; others examine the history and theory of research methodology overall. The breadth and depth of experience of faculty teaching these courses means that I have numerous professors to whom I can turn if I have a methodological question – many more than are on my committee. I have had Skype and email conversations with professors while in the field that have been invaluable in helping me move my dissertation research forward.

I am part of several informal support networks. First, I belong to a dissertation writing group made up of students from different universities and departments but who are all writing QRDs in the same substantive area (thankfully not on the exact same topic!). Over the past two and a half years, this group has met regularly over Skype and conducted dozens of email conversations; we constructively critique each other's work and provide general support.

I am also part of a group of graduate students who are all conducting research in the same field site. Our group varies widely in terms of substantive focus and disciplinary background, but we are all conducting QDs. We meet regularly for dinner and use our time together to discuss fieldwork issues – both the positive aspects and the tribulations that come from conducting extended research in a foreign country.

5. *What methodological questions were raised by your work? How did you answer them?* One methodological question I reflect upon regularly has to do with the match between my methods and my epistemology and a meta-theoretical approach. I am a strong believer in conducting research using feminist principles, yet on a daily basis, as I discuss various issues in my interviews and/or present myself in certain ways to my participants, I ask myself whether the questions I raise or the way that I ask them is in line with the principles I believe are important. This is a matter of being constantly vigilant about putting ideals into practice.

6. *Thesis appearance?* I haven't completed it yet!

7. *Are there any stories you would like to share?* During data collection, I was unable to be at the group's meeting one week. In talking with the group leader, it seems the members asked where I was, a question that led into what was apparently a very interesting discussion about what I was doing and how the group members felt about it. The leader told me that a few members mentioned feeling a bit intimidated by my presence with a notebook; one, apparently, said she felt a bit like a "lab rat."

Now, I spoke with the group before I began my observations and explained to them what I was doing there, what types of topics I was interested in learning about, etc. The group was also provided with written informed consent forms that provided a fuller explanation of my research and observation procedures. Yet, clearly my presence, even with their permission, has influenced (in negative or positive ways, I can't know) the group dynamics.

I tell this story not so much as a word of caution but rather to engender some reflection about qualitative 'data.' In particular, this experience made concrete to me how qual data do not reflect a single, objective reality. Data, at the most fundamental level, are co-constructed through the experiences of the researcher and research participants: what results embodies only one of many realities. Hope this helps. Karen R.

## METHODOLOGY

Participant case study seemed to alarm the committee. **Mary** had to be very explicit with design and methods in order to convince them this would be "valid" dissertation work. The biggest effort was put into researcher bias questions.

**Joan** utilized Flanagan's (1954) critical incident technique (CIT), an exploratory, QR method that generates descriptive data. It provides a structured yet flexible data collection method for producing a thematic or categorical representation of a given behavior or its components. I had questions about emergent themes, coding, and how grounded theory evolved from the data. I tackled these issues by reading the works of Johnson and Fauske (2000); and Redman, Lambrecht, and Stitt-Golden (2000). Additionally, one of my co-chairs has authored numerous qual articles, studies, and research. She served as my "guidepost".

Gradually, **Wanju** became more confident in conducting QR projects. My adviser, Dr. Klaus Witz is a strong advocate for "the participant as ally" and the essentialist portraiture approach (Witz, 2006). With his guidance, I completed an early research project titled, "How a Teacher Unfolds in Teaching." I conducted eight, one-to-two hour interviews with my participant and wrote a 50-page portrait of her.

The writing process was truly labor-intensive. However, I felt all of my hard work paid off when I received comments from readers who asked, "Were you a novelist before you did QR?" This comment made me feel that I was able to present my participant vividly. Through my words, her teaching experience and stories came alive.

I used the same research methodology to conduct my dissertation, however, I had five participants for this project. For each one I wrote a 10 to 15 page portrait. (See Appendix III)

The most exciting part of **Angela F**'s dissertation was being able to develop a constructivist methodology for understanding the representation of change, which I accomplished through the support and encouragement of my advisor and then through a grounded process for creating the methodology.

**Sharon**'s goal necessitated the development of a methodology that would allow me to collect data that gave my case a depth of understanding of what multicultural awareness looked like to the student residents and whether or not they felt that the process of education – implemented by faculty-in-resident programmed events and activities – was accessible in their residential environment on campus.

**Donna,** *challenged by her son to study men working in the profession of nursing,* thinks one difficult aspect of the research was in the seeming contradiction of the study; I felt as though I had to constantly justify myself. Being able to pull out a survey or a questionnaire seemed much more civilized than conducting face to face interviews with men I had never met.

Some of the participants I approached for the study were reluctant to meet with me; access to men who worked in nursing was a complex negotiation. I quickly learned to build a network of access.... Entry in the field was a thorny process for me, a critical feminist researcher studying masculinity. At times, I acutely felt like an outsider to my own study.

## DATA COLLECTION

**Debra** *is certain there* is a special Murphy's Law when it comes to conducting QR, which includes such events as blizzards, illnesses, car trouble, faulty travel directions, inadequate road signage, and unexpected traffic jams/detours. Or, everyone makes it, on time, and it proceeds beyond your wildest dreams when, just as you are about to wrap up, you discover that your tape recorder wasn't recording, because you hit the wrong button or your batteries went dead. Needless to say, while this situation can result in surprising yourself about the number of swear words that you know (and in languages you weren't even aware that you spoke!), it has potential consequences for staying on track with your data collection plan.

**Monica Jean** not only had trouble contacting participants and dealing with a hurricane, which postponed some of my data collection efforts, but also trying to find a way of presenting the data that was acceptable to both me and my committee members. Unexpected things will happen, this is a given. It's the way you deal with them that matters; be able to roll with the punches.

At first **Roxanne** tried to make sure I met with each of my participants in person for their life history analysis. But it became difficult to find time to interview 26 individuals at a specific location. So I began doing some of the interviews by phone. I know some would argue that body language cannot be read and rapport cannot be established, but it was an issue of timing and making the interviews/scheduling easier for my participants; I felt it was the right decision.

**Cindy**'s biggest methodological concern was the language barrier. I hired a translator to travel with me for the one month of my data collection. She was an English teacher in one of the 11 community colleges in my study and had been in the U.S. the previous year to earn a certificate at the college that employed me full-time. There was a relationship of trust between us. She translated my surveys into

Vietnamese and "tested" them on Vietnamese, Vietnamese to make sure the meaning of the questions translated across cultures. She translated the surveys at night in the hotel rooms we shared. This allowed her to ask me questions and me to question her translations to make sure I understood, across culture, the subject's response.

INTERVIEWS

**Debra** realizes conducting QR that results in insightful data relies on so many different factors, many of which you cannot control or will not know about until you are in the middle of data collection. For example, the interview protocol that seemed so well-crafted on paper only may elicit "yes" or "no" answers. Or, the person being interviewed misunderstands the concept you are asking about or flat out doesn't understand a question.

I also learned that there are potential issues related to credibility, rapport, and mood. Your questions may be well-crafted and the interviewee may understand the concepts. But, he or she may be shy or just in no mood to talk, either at all, or, just to you. Or, you have interviewees who are in a surly frame of mind because they detest the context that has created the need for the interview in the first place; they not only want to talk, but they also want to make sure that you fully understand their stance, rather than answering your questions. I once interviewed ...; keeping this individual focused on the questions at hand was quite a chore.

Even when your participants are eager to answer your questions and are enthusiastic about the purpose of your study, I learned that they may not be able to give you the promised amount of time due to unanticipated circumstances. This is not unusual when your research takes place in a school or child care setting. It seemed like my data collection visits always were accompanied by staffing shortages, fire drills, and children that needed to be calmed down and/or spoken to by the same individual I was trying to interview. While unanticipated events were stress inducing at the time, they also have been useful for teaching me the value of preparing for inevitable, unanticipated events. You may not be able to control such events, but you can add extra days and participants to your proposal.

**Sharon** used semi-structured interviewing as a research method for the pre- and post-workshop student resident participant interviews and faculty-in-residence interviews. Additionally, my advisor and I co-facilitated a multicultural awareness education workshop as a part of my research design to gain greater depth of understanding how students perceived multicultural education in their residential environment.

**Carin** asserts that the interview training I had helped me feel more comfortable setting the stage for the interviews and building rapport. I felt more at ease waiting for answers, in what can feel like a long period of silence. I learned the craft of saying less, allowing interviewees to share their experiences and meaning of them. I became more aware of the importance of short and simple follow-up/probing questions designed to keep the interviewee talking, e.g., tell me more/in what ways/ why/what was that like? And how so/how did you handle that/how did it affect you?

**Isabelle** guessed that because of my accent my participants would know right away I was French. I feared they would not be completely honest when I interviewed them, that they would give me answers they thought were politically correct or inoffensive to me. I had to find a way to keep the format and spontaneity of an interview but without the participants hearing my voice. Technology helped me!!! How I wish twitter had existed at the time I collected data! For my needs, I chose instant messenger; it provided anonymity on both sides and as an added bonus, instant transcripts of the conversations.

The second methodological question **Jim O** had was *where* my interviews should take place. I decided to rent a small office close to the campus and conducted some of my interviews there. However, most of my interviews were conducted in the participants' homes/apartments. This proved to be extremely beneficial as it gave me access to many personal details that I would not have been privy to otherwise. I was able to ask questions about family photos and other artifacts that held meaning to my participants and increased the depth of my understanding.

**Liz** wasn't as good with taking notes while interviewing so I adopted the strategy of recording (with permission and IRB approval, of course) and/or dictating additional notes and recollections immediately after the interview ends. But when it came to synthesizing it – really understanding how to identify patterns and building up into themes, well, my project grade illustrated that particular weakness. So I knew I had my work cut out for me as I began the dissertation.

**Keith** *also found data collection* to be somewhat problematic. *With his approval, I have edited several paragraphs he submitted whole from Chapter 3 of his dissertation and then continue with his reflection.*

Over the course of the 3-month fieldwork, the clean methodological plan outlined in the beginning of the chapter, ironically, became one of the largest hurdles. I was trapped in a conceptual box of formal protocol, which had the potential of undermining…the critical nature of this study … (p. 66)

My second interview proved to be the revelation. I felt it was productive; Bryce seemed much more at ease. At the close of the interview, Bryce made a remark that quite literally stopped me in my tracks.

"You know, all this time, I thought you were a shrink."

I asked him why.

He said he was not quite sure; that perhaps my questions gave him the vibe of someone trying to dissect him.

In one sentence Bryce pointed out to me a simple fact: the formal interviews were limiting our interactions and the data. I wondered if the participants, given the setting they are in, were sensitive to scrutinizing adults who probed their lives. I realized the inherently limiting aspects of the traditional question and answer interview in this setting, reinforcing the need for open, flexible, and pragmatic considerations in the inquiry methods I had imagined and chosen (Patton, 2002). (From p. 69 of my dissertation)

**Keith** *continues:* More importantly, I reflected on the interviews from which I thought I was getting "good" data. In those "good" interviews, I had latched on to phrases such as "need art to calm me down" or "writing is like my drug." Yet, the abrupt reminder of the lack of trust or comfort forced me to rethink those "good" answers. I recognized the clichéd nature of their responses and began to wonder: Were they stock answers? Did the participants respond that way because that was the expectation? By using those statements as data excerpts, would I, in some way, perpetuate a stigma of a troubled student and artistic processes as a one-size fits all hopes at redemption for that student? As you can see, I attempted to use a critical lens to interpret my own study. I encourage you to revisit what you consider as "good" data; more importantly, be critical of the context in which such "good" data emerges. Sometimes we graduate students get so caught up on the degree, the committee members, and any other external motivator that we may overlook or inadvertently manipulate the most important part of our research: the participants' voice.

Although **Carita** had two classes that introduced me to QR, I still felt like I was in uncharted territory as I worked with my own data. During each step of the process, I wanted to be authentic both with the students I was interviewing and to the QR process.

DATA ANALYSIS AND THEORETICAL FRAMEWORKS

A number of challenges accompanied **Angela LV**'s experience as a doctoral student. Many are still present after having completed the dissertation. One big challenge was to tell the story of my data under the lens of a theoretical framework. When reading published studies, it was easy to see how authors related theory, analysis, and data. It was not that easy when I had to do it myself! During the writing phase of my dissertation, it became clearer that a constant dialogue between the theoretical framework and the analysis had to exist so that finding construction could take place. I knew from my advisor that the theoretical framework had to guide the data analysis; this did not make sense until I had to make analytical choices myself to produce my findings.

In the midst of data analysis, I more vividly realized the presence of aspects and nuances of my initially chosen theoretical framework, as well as the need for an additional theoretical idea that could explain the choices I was making. For instance, I realized that the socio-cultural theories that were fundamental to analyze the school- and home-based literacy practices were insufficient when it came to understand what the children did when they read text in English and in Spanish. To analyze these data, I needed the help of cognitive theories of reading. I found myself going back and forth between the theoretical framework and the findings section, refining my theoretical supports as new insights from the data emerged.

> **Chad** Timm*'s letter, below, clearly explicates the thinking and doing related to data collection, interpretation, theory connecting and building.*

Dear Judy: I conducted a critical ethnography of a partnership between a grassroots, community based organization and an urban public school system. The purpose of the partnership was to simultaneously help families leave poverty and improve their children's academic achievement.

Shortly after I began fieldwork I noticed that the middle class allies, community organizers, and school officials sought to "teach" these families living in poverty how to be middle class. The purpose of the weekly meeting, where everyone would gather for dinner and discussion about important academic, financial, or community-building issues, was to help participant families learn to budget more effectively or emphasize education in their homes. These meetings, therefore, often reinforced the dominant stereotypes of the poor. As a result, the participant families were constantly confronted with stereotypes and exaggerations. What made my analysis complicated, however, was that I began to see that there was a tension or a conflict emerging, which was that the community organizer at one time lived in poverty. She collected welfare for a time but was now comfortably middle class.

During the meetings she often referred to her own experiences of living in poverty. On one occasion I wrote in my research journal, "I felt that Sara did a good job tonight talking about community activities. Sara is very good at relating her own life history, and her struggle with bad credit and poverty, to the participants." During the meetings Sara often referred to the structural barriers that she and the participant families faced, like lack of affordable childcare, housing, health insurance, or a living wage. In these moments the middle class allies and school officials saw that in many ways leaving poverty had as much, if not more, to do with overcoming institutional injustices than the personal will or choice to take a different path.

So what does this have to do with analysis? I was confused, that's the bottom line. Sara simultaneously reinforced the dominant discourse and spoke back to it. She helped to teach participant families how to "be middle class," but also tried to teach the allies that poverty was the result of systemic failings. I initially believed that Sara possessed some kind of a conflicted consciousness that resulted in a tension that needed to be overcome. I was convinced that Sara used her personal experience as a way to give her credibility among the participant families. I mean, she had been there and done that. Because I struggled to make sense of these observations I sought guidance from theory. My searching first led me to the work of Pierre Bourdieu, who describes how people can possess forms of cultural capital that give them authority in certain situations. According to Bourdieu's (1986; 1996) theorizations, Sara was relying on her personal experiences of living in poverty as a form of cultural capital that gave her credibility among the participants in the program. This explanation, however, didn't quite fit.

Sara certainly possessed dominant cultural capital: she knew how to apply for an interview for a job, budget effectively, speak "proper" English, and so on. What made Sara different, however, was that she also possessed the cultural capital of a person who had lived in poverty. She knew the struggles, the barriers, and among other things the ways to negotiate the social service system, something the allies and school officials knew nothing about. Bourdieu's (1986) work didn't help me to understand how cultural capital could be non-dominant. Here was a person using a form of cultural capital in order to gain credibility that wasn't validated by dominant society.

My next step was to find other theorists who used Bourdieu but theorized about how cultural capital could be non-dominant. Using QR, both Carter (2003) and Yosso (2005) describe how cultural capital can be non-dominant and how non-dominant or marginalized communities possess capital that isn't validated by mainstream society. With my new knowledge of dominant and non-dominant forms of capital I returned to my data. Remember, at first I believed Sara, the community organizer, had to have a conflicted consciousness because she seemed to both advocate for the poor and try to impose her middle class views on them. By wrestling with the theory and going back to my data, engaging in an intensely reflexive process whereby I repeatedly read and re-read the data through the lens of Bourdieu and those who added to his theorizations, I literally had an epiphany. I remember my dissertation advisor telling me that eventually themes would emerge from my data analysis. Frankly, I was beginning to doubt her; it was like looking at one of those 3-D pictures from the 1980s, where you had to let your eyes go out of focus until you finally saw the unicorn or dolphin jumping out of the water. These pictures used to frustrate me so much; the harder I looked at the image, the longer it took me to see it. In the case of my dissertation, I looked hard at the data, looked hard at the theory, and finally stepped back, letting my eyes go out of focus for a minute, and I saw the data differently.

Instead of a conflicted conscience, Sara possessed both dominant and non-dominant forms of capital. As a matter of fact, everyone in the program, from school officials to participant families, were constantly confronting and negotiating and learning about both dominant and non-dominant forms of capital. What was happening at these meetings was that everyone in attendance was occupying a space not of just dominance or non-dominance, but a space between. I had it! I finally saw that instead of a conflict, there was a space of possibility. I returned to theory and researched theorists who described situations where dominant and non-dominant groups, and their ideas, occupied the same spaces. Postcolonial theorist Bhabha (1985) describes what happens in the colonial encounter when the colonizer seeks to colonize the "other." In these moments Bhabha contends the colonizer is never completely successful, as there is always a Third Space that emerges between the discourse of the colonizer and the colonized. This Third Space is a space of potential, where the colonized can re-define and re-interpret the discourse of the colonizer.

I then took Bourdieu (1986; 1996) informed by Carter (2003) and Yosso (2005), and added Third Space theory and found that what was occurring in the encounters I was witnessing was a Third Space moment. While community organizers, school officials, and middle class volunteers sought to "teach" families living in poverty how to be middle class, the participant families were teaching the organizers and allies about what it meant to be poor in a society that allowed and encouraged poverty. While participant families were learning about how to interview for a job, they were teaching their allies about a job market that did not pay them living wages. Using my understandings of capital and Third Space, I theorized a new form of capital was developed during these encounters, what I referred to as 'liberatory' capital. If the meetings would have only taught participant families how to be middle class they would have been simply oppressing a marginalized group with a dominant discourse. If the meetings had only validated and recognized the participant's non-dominant capital, the participant families would not have learned the pragmatic skills necessary to budget more effectively or acquire the skills to find a higher paying job. But, if both dominant and non-dominant forms of capital were simultaneously validated in these meetings, participants could acquire the pragmatic skills while their allies learned of the structural barriers to leaving poverty.

I felt very much like Alice tumbling down the rabbit hole. When I finally came out, I had developed theory that didn't exist before. Best wishes, Chad


## DATA ANALYSIS

Although **Isabelle** did a preliminary analysis of the data, I did not look for themes. I just went over each interview before I did the next to see what was said and to build onto the next interview. Once data collection was over and I started analyzing, I realized that I had to rethink my approach. I had hypothesized that there would be differences in stereotypes due to background. I had intended to present a mixed-methods analysis of my findings, which would include correlations between gender and stereotypes or previous years of language study and stereotypes, but it turned out there were no differences. I had to go qual all the way with some descriptive numbers. I had to rethink my entire data analysis and most importantly my coding procedures. So I adapted. I learned that with research, the key word is flexibility in thinking and adaptability in practice.

**Roxanne** definitely had A LOT of data that required me to be very organized. I had to put my thoughts and the voice of my participants into memos to help me frame my analysis.

During the data analysis phase, **Cindy** often felt overwhelmed with the mountains of data I had collected. The best advice I had received at that phase was, "Take little steps; every day spend at least an hour working on the dissertation." I devised my own data organization plan by reading several textbook chapters on the topic. I visualized how I might organize the mountains of paper and electronic files and then visited an office supply store for several hours to purchase the best tools I could find to bring my vision to reality.

**Cassandra**'s methodologist had used analytic induction in some of her own research; she was comfortable with it and favored the procedure. I, on the other hand, originally thought the analytic induction process was too complicated and did not want to have anything to do with it.

I did not agree to incorporate the procedure into my research until after I struggled for days trying to make sense of the ton of transcribed data I had in front of me. I will say I had some very restless nights when I first started the process. But as I kept going over what I was attempting to do, it began to take shape. First I formulated two hypotheses about the nature and degree of entrepreneurship shown in the study participants. Then I formulated themes that allowed me to examine the essence (or nature) and degree of entrepreneurship of the study population—college leadership. Subsequently, I was able to describe my findings and "tell" my story more succinctly as a result of using analytic induction.

**Veronica** thought I would do what others in the field have done, that is, a thematic analysis focused on emerging themes. What I did not realize is that the methodological plan I set forth would guide me from data collection, to analysis, and, finally, to representation. Similar to what Lawrence-Lightfoot (1983) did in *The Good High School*, I highlighted each case/participant individually. I deliberately selected excerpts from the data, both visual, i.e., photographs from photo-elicitation interviewing processes, and written, i.e., interview transcriptions that (1) fit the (Re) valuing Methodology categories I had established, and (2) gave value to each of the novice teachers, their content, their pedagogical practices, and their literacy understandings. The result was individual portraits, representing each participant's journey through the research, a journey of initial understandings, content area literacy lesson planning, teaching, and reflecting on meaning-making processes, with concluding understandings and areas of growth. The basic structure of the portraits included three main divisions and related subdivisions aligning with (Re) valuing Methodological processes.

Something that helped **Michele** immensely was talking with others about what I was finding. I kept a notebook of my thoughts and found that some ideas returned over and over. I decided those interpretations must be important. Writing random thoughts was also helpful; they often came in the middle of the night. It also helped to work on other parts of the dissertation when I felt perplexed by the analysis. When I came back to it after a few days, things seemed clearer.

**Donna** learned volumes about analyzing qual data through my study. After the interviews were transcribed, peer checked, and read through twice, I chunked the data into categories; soon themes began to emerge. I took huge sheets of post-it butcher paper and copied direct quotes from the interviews onto the categories. Initially, there must have been about 12 or so categories. To really "live" with my data, I posted them on the walls of my dining room. I would spend hours walking around the room reading their words and moving quotes as categories collapsed and themes began to take form.

A compelling category was "identity" in which all of the men told stories that centered them as the hero. Consistent tales of, "I was known as the best shot giver in the hospital!" (p. 134) or "We fought the trauma monsters and the trauma demons!" (p.143) resounded through every interview. The men used phrases like, "adrenaline junkie" (p. 134) and "go-to guy" (p.134) to describe themselves. At first read, I thought the men were bragging; this must be an aspect of "performance" in the interview process, and they were trying to impress me. My initial analysis was the participants used heroic words and phrases in an effort to define their experiences as standing out or excelling within the female majority.

After a few weeks of living with data plastered on every wall in my dining room, one early morning I was stumbling through to get a coffee and I looked at the words on the sheet containing all quotes of, what I previously had assumed to be, bravado. Suddenly, I got it! These men were not bragging to me; they fully realized that they were not fulfilling societal expectations of a career suitable for a man. These words were a badge declaring that *they* were not a part of a marginalized minority. I was witnessing how these men managed their concept of masculinity in a female-dominated occupation and realized they related these vignettes of heroism in which they held expertise apart from their female peers in the profession to convince me (themselves?) that even though there are not many men in nursing, and they had not followed a societal sex-role appropriate occupation, they were good at what they did. They made a difference. Every aspect of their lives were affected because they worked in nursing, from relationships with their families, to struggles with peers, doctors, and conflicting societal messages of masculine identity (p. 195). It was a revelation as I finally felt that I was able to empathically understand what they were trying to convey.

WHAT NEXT?

**Francesca** suggests that just because you find something does not mean you have to report on it. I found a lot of interesting results that did not go to my research questions. In this case, I put them aside and had to realize that although they were not good for this particular project, I could use them in the future.

**Anabella** asks how do you ensure that in the final presentation of your research you represent the diversity in the data? When I completed the data collection and verification process (checking all transcriptions against the original recordings) I recall thinking, "Okay, how do I pull this all together?" I wasn't so much worried about summarizing and synthesizing the data, but more so about including all of my participants' voices in the data summaries that would later be turned into data claims. An analysis question, it had to do with how I pulled the data into its different parts, understood these parts in themselves and then what construct or common thread would I use to integrate them.

When engaging in data analysis the researcher strives to find commonalities in order to provide a picture of how the subjects make sense of the topic at hand. What happens when you cannot find that commonality, when each individual provides a unique perspective that is valuable in itself? I addressed this by looking at each individual's perspectives as contributing information/insight to the broader process I was studying. I was no longer concerned about including all the data but more about including data that constituted an important piece to understanding that process.

I learned that QR is a process very much guided by the researcher's intuitiveness and capacity to manage data analysis at different levels. Emphasizing intuition does not throw out the window the theoretical underpinnings of QR or the procedures that stem from these. On the contrary, it raises their significance in the sense that to ensure the rigor and validity of the study the researcher's intuitiveness must be informed by such underpinnings and procedures. The ability of a qual researcher to face the issues that surge in the development of a QR project rests on his/her capacity to address them, taking into consideration the tenets and principles of QR but also the nature of the project itself. For example, one does not find cookie cutter answers in the research methodology literature of what to do when access to your site is compromised half-way through the data collection? If the lit does provide a response, the researcher must assess if that is the best approach for the situation.

At the end it is a decision that is significantly based on your gut feeling, on your instinct as someone interested in understanding more about a certain topic of study and figuring out, many times on the spot, what is the best way to go about it. The important lesson for me is that undertaking QR implies trusting your instinct and realizing that at this point in your academic trajectory it is not that "basic"; that it has been informed by a series of scholarly experiences that will guide you in the process.

CONCLUSION

One of the things I am trying to do with this book is to go back and forth from attention to aspects of the work to the whole of the experience as shared with me through the correspondents' letters; hence, I decided to place **Rosaire**'s letter below. (I describe the importance of this letter to my own analysis in Appendix I.) While you may be interested at the moment in "this" or "that", you must realize I am reminding you about the layered interconnectivity of learning by doing.

I remember concluding my first presentation at the American Educational Research Association (1986, I think?!) with a statement sounding something like: 'Although we are just a bit of the whole of our participants' lives, they become a whole in the experiencing of ours'. I have become a wiser teacher for consciously acknowledging the 'whole' of my students' lives, and I hope a better author for offering you some "whole" of individual experiences – and individuals – as they shared themselves and their thinking with me.

*An Interview with* **Rosaire** Ifedi *(abridged)*

*What was the best thing about your course work,* Rosaire? Qualitative inquiry was one of my core courses. My professor, who later became a member of my dissertation committee, is a renowned author and postmodernist qual researcher. The course offered some life changing experiences. I got to try out QR by conducting a pilot study. I look back and still see that project as one of the best things that prepared me for the doctoral dissertation.

*What was it about the pilot study that affected you?* At that point in my life, I was working in correctional education. It was here I found my problem, just as Merriam (2009) says, we just need to open our eyes to see them. This assignment was the beginning of my foray into lived experiences. Van Manen (1990) would later become a bedside companion in the dissertation production.

My pilot study was a phenomenological exploration. It was an appetizer of experiencing the saliences of emic and etic perspectives, the ambiguities of being a primary instrument, the pros of interviewing and the failures of observation methods, the paucity of research in some areas and even the "so what?" of research. I lived first-hand the emergent nature of QR. By the time I concluded this study, I had seen so much of myself that I had probably been afraid to confront earlier. I recall phrasing the experience of analyzing the data as looking in the mirror. As I engaged with the accounts of the participants, I was in a sense looking at their information but also seeing myself in the themes that emerged. I had begun with a "so what?" and ended with a "Now what?" The findings of the study impacted me enough to make a career change.

*So what did happen next,* **Rosaire**? One of my mentors, who later became my committee chair, asked me to co-teach a QR class with her.

*What were you thinking about QR at the time? Did you have a topic yet?* I found the paradigm more meaningful, authentic, and relevant in exploring the more complex issues of our messy lives. Patti Lather and Chris Smithies' (1997) "Troubling the Angels" became a powerful symbol in understanding what we seek and therefore how we seek it the qual way.

I was also settled in my mind about the kinds of questions I wanted to ask – naturalistic, contextual, and authentic. However, I was not settled on the specific topic. Here's where one practical tip helped: talk and share! The members of my cohort shared dissertation topics, questions, and ideas. As soon as I shared some of my thoughts, several peers grabbed on to the idea of African-born women, like me, and our experiences. I must have sounded more fascinating than I possibly could have been, but those few classmates found my story intriguing enough to think it would make for good research! Essentially, they helped me move towards this area of study.

*You write that next came the "so what" question? Before you even had a topic?* Yes. Even if these few enamored classmates thought I could tell this story, I battled with who else would want to know about African-born professors? It took weeks – and a reassurance that research is about contributing whatever is missing to the knowledge base – for me to decide. When I began my LR, it hit me immediately that there was little to nothing about this specific population. It helped me to know that since I didn't know what I would find, I needn't worry too much about what findings would emerge and what implications there would be. I was a confident novice researcher as I plugged on at this stage, comfortable with the process and totally open to new understandings. I continued to teach the QR course as an adjunct to masters' students, which turned out to be another valuable resource. I could understand their frustrations while reinforcing my own methodological skills.

*Okay,* Rosaire. *You are feeling confident; now what? You seem to be thinking about yourself related to your participants in several ways?*　That is correct. I had begun to collect data. Keeping a journal, being honest to the process, and reflecting on my reflexivity were all invaluable iterative steps that made this process work for me. For instance, I journaled questions, bracketing them as I collected data, particularly if a participant's story seemed incredulous to me. I also looked at the participants' websites, etc.

Fine et al. (2003) remind us not to hide "behind [a] cloak of alleged neutrality" (p. 169). This one statement became a mantra for me. I have repeatedly referred to it, letting it guide my ethics of research. Doing so allowed me to see myself both honestly as an insider and outsider to my study.

More importantly, that sense of honesty and looking for meaning shaped my selection of a theoretical framework. One is looking always to see what others have done and follow it, in accordance with research protocol and validity standards. However, finding support for themes is in tense competition with creativity and novelty, and ultimately, knowledge creation. How do I not lose my voice and creativity even with the methods I choose or the theoretical framework I adopt? One of the members of my committee commented to me months into the lit review process that I needed to adopt my theoretical framework *before* getting too far ahead. That comment was a life saver!

*Are you saying you need to select a theoretical framework that would address/allow your honesty – and your participants' – to be heard?*　I had encountered critical race theory. In looking at lives of women who I assumed may have issues about race, the theory was a right fit. Nonetheless, I had also encountered stories of resilience from minority professors of African American, Asian and Caribbean backgrounds. The search for meaning was not being framed by only one theory. Then I encountered Denzin and Lincoln's (2003) theoretical and methodological *bricoleur*. In my thesis I wrote:

> The key for me in choosing theoretical frameworks was to appeal to whatever…
> spoke to, highlighted, and validated the experiences of the participants as

immigrant faculty women of color. Because one paradigm was insufficient to address their lived realities, a tapestry of frameworks was used. (p. 74)

**Rosaire,** *we are still talking about 'subjectivities' and assumptions?* Yes. I find it useful that we surface our subjectivities in particular locations of our end product. Here's a story of how as I began to analyze the data; I surfaced my experiences and found myself, in a literal sense, in a dance with my participants and the data they gave me.

> I realized I was engaged in a phenomenological dance with my co-researchers or participants. Every time I asked a question and they began to answer, I found myself sometimes stepping in to relive the experience and sometimes stepping out to behold as in a mirror another reflection of the experience. I had to exercise fluidity as outsider and insider. When one of the participants describes her excitement at voting for the first time as a U.S. citizen, I relived that experience with her as I had just become a citizen myself. However, I had not experienced the tenure process, so I listened as an outsider to all the participants' accounts.
>
> When I began to analyze the data, that dance continued. Sometimes when I read their answers, they became the primary investigator of the experience while I stepped away and listened. ... I was reading the transcripts for data, but the participants investigated the phenomenon. It was an intriguing experience and when it happened a number of times, I went back to my notes on methodology and to the experts and was even more confounded when some of the authors re-explained, reconfirmed and revalidated my experience with methods and analysis. (pp. 95–96)

Rosaire, *you found what I have found! You-all are leading this book's emergence and form. But may I ask you to be more specific about coding and learning from our data?* When it comes to findings and themes, I analyzed my data using both themes in literature and in the raw data. Doing so brought the challenge of encountering data and findings that ran contrary to accepted views or other research. When it happens, we must then be brave enough to face what in the data counters our biases. It is in the honesty of this process that the power of QR lies. There is nothing to hide.

Novice researchers may tend to ignore, discount or belittle such data and findings. I have learned not to do so as sometimes those new questions and answers that are raised prove to be the most significant. My dissertation chair was particularly supportive as she encouraged me to stand by my findings.

*I would like to go back to your "mirror" analogy,* Rosaire; *if I am understanding your letter, you are suggesting that a qual researcher encounters him/herself across many points of the QR journey? Where in the final document are you more explicit about this experience?*    The third area to surface and integrate my prior knowledge and understanding is the Discussion section. While the theoretical framework helped me to interpret, report, and categorize my findings to make sense of them, the Discussion allowed me to make even more sense of it. It proved to be a closure, a settling of some of the "discordant themes". Rosaire

*Below,* **Lisa W** *makes explicit one of the* unexpected *conclusions experienced qualitative researchers regularly come to expect, while Mary offers a glimpse of hope! It makes sense to pause here, ending part two.*

One of the research questions I thought might be answered did not have as much meaning once I finished coding and analyzing the data. However, I did find that while it did not result in much collective sensemaking, several individuals told me it caused them to think or engage in individual sensemaking. They did feel that it affected their professional identity. I guess it was a lesson for me to learn that although what I thought would happen, didn't, something else did, and that was an important result to my study. I guess I am saying here that I learned a great deal about the process, and what I thought would/might occur and be important needed to be examined, but that I shouldn't overlook other things that occur even though I hadn't thought about them in the beginning.

What **Mary** learned from the struggle to come to some conclusions was not only fear of failure but more importantly the joy of thinking! As I kept at it and reread, and referred back to methodological references and the literature in my three conceptual areas, my interest and 'passion' remained and my curiosity to see what comes from all of this sustained me.

# STILL INTO IT

**Angela LV:** In other words, the methods literature falls short on describing what a "systematic analysis" looks like when the analytical clear-cut steps become blurred by the "story" that emerges from the data.

## INTRODUCTION

As you have gathered from the variety and depth of responses so far in Section Two, the "doing" of QR is the location of the learning. Data analysis is certainly a major challenge.

## DATA ANALYSIS (CONTINUED)

**Angela LV**'s *conclusion above introducing the third part of Section Two, needs to be prefaced by the following*:

All the QM textbooks point out the importance of "systematically analyzing the data" to ensure the reliability of the findings. I always interpreted the "systematic" as meaning to have a premeditated plan for analysis, sticking to it, and submitting all the data to the same plan. This interpretation was reinforced by the dissertation proposal defense, where a plan for data collection and analysis needed to be clearly laid out, even without yet having the data for the study. The problem with thinking of data analysis as a preplanned number of uniform analytical procedures – as I later realized – was that such an approach alone was insufficient.

At the onset of data analysis, I pledged faithfulness to systematicity, dedicating my best efforts on trying to apply clear-cut and orderly steps to all my data. I read once, coded once, and did not do anything else until I finished coding that batch of data. Then I revisited all the data to refine my codes. In the name of "systematicity" I abstained from pursuing any sudden insights if they were "outside" of the analytical "step" I was making. Unconsciously, maybe, I was expecting that by making all the systematic analytical "moves" the findings would "form" themselves entirely from my codes and themes, and all I had to do was use them as titles and then write the finding that derived from them!

Many times I refrained from embracing the stories I saw emerge in my data for fear of not being "systematic" enough with my approach. Having a large number of codes, and later a number of themes resulting from categorizing the codes was an important part of getting familiarized with all sources of data, but the codes and themes were not the FINDINGS. They were ideas, possibilities, details, and many times, unimportant episodes that somehow got inflated by looking too closely to one event. Much more conceptual work was needed to make the "systematic analysis" evolve into actual findings. I realized that major conceptual developments needed to occur at the same time that I coded, recoded, and synthesized the codes into themes. Without making more complex interconnections throughout the data, the findings section of my dissertation would still be in my to-do list.

I realized that the QM books could only take me so far, and that I would have to figure out the rest on my own. All books presented systematicity as an absolute condition to apply to all the data. They did not discuss the limitations and challenges of being systematic when places of interconnection started surfacing for some of the data only.

**Jim O** remembers the amount of confusion I experienced when I began looking for the "best" way to code my data and do thematic analyses. After reading a number of sources on the subject, it appeared to me that there was no "lock-step" process for coding. Being somewhat structuralist in my approach to most things in life, this was extremely frustrating because it required me to place a certain amount of "faith" in my abilities and the ultimate personal approach I used. In hindsight, I can now appreciate that experience because I believe it made me grow as a qualitative researcher, and also as a professional.

As **Ellie** used multiple case studies about a family, it was important to have outside reviewers look at my data and analysis objectively. Constant feedback and collaboration with genuine interest in research helped me to work on the enormous amount of data.

## TO TRANSCRIBE OR NOT TO TRANSCRIBE?

**Carin** had notable financial support; a combination of institutional and departmental funds paid for most of the transcription, which was in my mind the best way to spend my limited allocation! I worked on my degree for 5½ years. I imagine it would have been much longer had I transcribed my own interviews.

**Jim O** chose to utilize a transcriptionist for my interviews. I was lucky to locate an extremely reasonable person for a fraction of what most others were quoting, but it was still rather taxing.

Because QR studies involve many interviews and observations, transcribing takes a lot of time, especially if you are not trained. When time is precious, it really is worth it to pay a transcriptionist. **Michelle** is applying for a grant to help cover the costs, because it can be pricey. But it is almost essential and very worth the money. Once **Kj** *and* **Monica** decided to have their data transcribed, the quality of life improved. **Monica** *had* painstakingly researched ways to tape telephone interviews; the transcription service suggested a call-in service that taped more clearly than the method I had come up with.

## CODING, CODING, CODING

**Cassandra** thinks coding is one area that Ph.D. programs and methodologists need to focus on. Even the simplest coding method is not easy to a novice researcher. Reading about coding and actually doing it are not one in the same. I asked my colleagues; we all struggled with the coding process.

If **Amy** were doing this again, I would have started my analysis earlier. When I was coding, there were cases arising that I would have liked to have gone back and observed for, but I didn't code until after data collection was complete (minus a few interviews).

The process of coding the interviews in Atlas took **Isabeau** WAAAAY more time than I thought; it was not very clear-cut. I figured that, after the coding I had done so meticulously, I would be able to produce an outline rather efficiently. Not so. Going over the codes took tons of time, too. I did this very thoroughly and further categorized information.

Had I not taken the course in qual data analysis, I might have worried that the not-straightforward process I am going through was 'abnormal.' Instead, I have gone into this phase knowing what to expect. I find it so rewarding that, through every phase, I am 'getting' a deeper understanding, making more links, etc. Now that I am writing, the analysis continues. Prior to the course, I had the impression things would be a lot more linear. And, they are not—but, that's okay! Phew!

The major question **Kj** had was, "What is the best way to analyze the data?" I came up with a process, or "system" of analyzing that was both methodical and made sense to me. It was based on discussions with my Chair, Dr. Britt, and reading Moustakas (1994) and Creswell's (2007) work on phenomenology.

1st -  Interview transcripts were open coded whereby emerging themes were highlighted.

2nd -  Observational field notes were open coded.

3rd -  Interview and observation themes were noted; major themes were recorded on a data grid.

4th -  Major themes were closed coded and grouped according to the three research questions.

5th -  After major themes from each participant were close coded, then participants' data as a group were analyzed for overall themes.

6th -  After themes for the participants as a whole were analyzed, the researcher followed the same process as steps one through five and analyzed her personal journal.

7th -  Major themes from the participants were placed onto 3x5 index cards and categorized into overall categories.

8th -  The categories were analyzed and placed according to which research question they addressed.

The statements and themes found throughout the open coding process became the basis for discussing the three research questions of my study. Remember to code, recode and give yourself time to reflect and just sit on the data for some time.

As **Lisa W** recalls, my methodological questions were resolved by numerous long conversations with my chair and mentor and included: What to do about participants who did not regularly attend the meetings? How to begin thinking about coding? How to make difficult coding choices? How to make sure I kept track of the coding choices made, and to make sure I was consistent in my decisions! So, coding was my biggest question; it was tedious but so exciting for me. I know my colleagues were wondering why I would get excited when leafing through pages of transcription; I would highlight to color code topics of conversation. The many hours spent filtering information in countless Excel spreadsheets was exhausting but invigorating.

> *I asked* **Alex** *to clarify his thinking related to coding, thinking his step by step description could be useful.*

I coded a large volume of media coverage of policy debates and in-depth interviews with about 40 policymakers and key stakeholders in two states to identify the frames used to debate charter schools, school choice, and accountability issues. I also coded the policy proposals being debated and identified the coalitions working for and against each iteration of the fight.

I created a framework that allows the analyst to identify whether the frames being used matched the dominant frame of the speaker's coalition, or whether they were using a modified version of a previous frame, or the negative version of the opponent's frame. I also identified these frames by three sub-components: the problem definition, supporting assumptions, and complementary policy solution of each frame. These three components tended to remain relatively constant, but …

Based on whether they used their own side's frames, or the opponent's, and whether they stuck with their coalition's policy positions in a series of policy votes, I coded the individual members of each coalition as ideologues, pragmatists, and dogmatic coalition members. I then examined whether a coalition's complexity (measured by the presence or frequency of all three types of actors and the number of frames they used), contributed to their victory. My hypothesis is that complex coalitions with actors that speak and behave differently, and that use different frames and take anomalous policy positions, win in the long run.

These steps seem very much like a QR project, but otherwise, these data were then used in an analysis that included a quant analysis of the actions in the states, the development of theory and conceptual frameworks, and the development and testing of hypotheses. My challenges were more about creating a framework and trying to identify concepts, like frames, in a way that I found amenable to systematic analysis.

My frustrations as a researcher in the academy were much greater around the issues of both qual and quant scholars being pretty clueless about how politicians actually behave and what they think. Political scientists simplify the political actors so badly that they can't imagine them as smart people acting in very complex, non-reduceable environments using tools that are hard to measure, like ideas and speech, to win in both short- and long-term rights.

***Amplification email.*** My coding method was a developmental issue for me, as I was trying to apply the conceptual framework I had developed for the project and then coding the text by that framework. My work and challenges were more about operationalizing a novel framework and figuring out the details of conceptual elements of my framework.

The text was often media quotes on a pending policy proposal, as well as interview transcripts. It was approached through an iterative coding approach. I coded for each statement:

1. the particular policy debate and year the statement was attributed to, so I could track the development of frames over time
2. whether the speaker to whom a statement was attributed was for or against a proposal in question
3. regardless of their position on the pending proposal, whether they were from a group that was historically from the pro- or anti- reform side of the debate

With questions 1, 2 and 3, I could identify as a speaker who was speaking against a proposal in a certain year, but who was from a group that traditionally supported the policy in other debates;

4. what frame they were using, using a similar set of frames if it was a reoccurring frame from this debate or previous debates, or a concise description if it was a frame that was new to the debate .

Once I could identify the frames being used in a debate and which side was using them, most often I could recode a frame as "the opposition's primary frame," or "the advocate's frame". These answers subsequently allowed me to code the statements by the framework I developed to identify whether the statement was offered by: pragmatic advocates, pragmatic opponents, ideological advocates, ideological opponents, or traditional advocates and traditional opponents.

The frequency and significance of the types of speakers within each coalition allowed me to characterize the degree of complexity or simplicity in the competing coalitions during that iteration. When a new frame emerged in the third iteration, I would attempt to track elements of the frame and try to identify, for each new/emerging frame:

1. its problem definition ("poor kids have few good choices")
2. a supporting view of the world ("civil rights orientation")
3. the linked solution indicated by the view ("target/justify new charters and choices for poor kids")

So, even when new frames emerged, the secondary analysis could identify if a problem definition or one of the other three elements of the frame was being borrowed from a previous frame in the earlier rounds. It sounds kind of complicated, but the framework provided a good structure, and the software, Nvivo, helped assign multiple codes to any single statement. Then I could print out the whole set of statements made across cases and iterations and compare and contrast according to the elements of the framework.

**Joan** did all my own transcribing and coding, which allowed me to become totally immersed in the data and data analysis.

TECHNOLOGY

**Bruce** suggests we discuss the use of technology. All of the QR projects I have worked on have used video data collection. In San Diego, we used Transana for transcription and analysis http://www.transana.org. My chair at Saint Mary's has recommended that I consider using Elan http://www.lat-mpi.eu/tools/elan/. There may be other similar products.

The issue freshest in **Isabeau**'s mind is the story I am going to tell. Sometime during the qual course, I decided I was going to do my analysis without any specialized qual-data computer software. I couldn't face the prospect of learning new software that seemed so complex (May 2010). Fast forward to August 2010: a faculty member-mentor (not someone on my committee) strongly urged me to consider Atlas.ti and provided strong arguments for doing so. I decided to explore it further. I sought the opinion of people in my network who had completed their Ph.Ds. and used it/a similar program. These were people I trusted a lot. They all gave me sound reasons for using it, so I decided to go ahead. During this time I had also consulted with my committee to see if any of them knew of people who might be able to help/advise me. Their response was not very helpful. My co-supervisors had not used the program. The 3rd committee member who had didn't offer to help me. So, once I made the decision to use Atlas, I then spent close to one month figuring out how to get it set up and use it. I have a Mac and Atlas needs a Windows platform. Thankfully, my mentor was able to help me get started. She hadn't used it for a long time but remembered enough to get me going.

I found this process somewhat draining because there was so little help. Plus, I am perfectly aware of how little I know about using the program, and that frustrates me. I get a sense of how powerful it is, but I use a microscopic aspect of it. I have accepted, at this point, that the rest of my learning about Atlas will come at a later stage.

**Mary** tried using software. I felt it was only marginally useful in interviews and not at all useful for questionnaire analysis. I changed the analysis to coding and sorting by hand. Later on, I unexpectedly found a good tool in the affordances of the NVivo software – the modeling tool visualized iterative steps that led me on to the most difficult part of the dissertation, i.e., coming to findings and conclusions for the final proposed model. My ability to use more labor intensive methods was enhanced by several strong presentations at national conferences. I particularly remember a Turkish professor demonstrating the use of Excel in analysis of qual data. Although I did not use his exact method, it served to widen my ideas and to encourage me that multiple methods are available.

**Vic** suggests that an MP3 splitter is invaluable as you work with the actual recordings.

By talking with colleagues, **Michelle** has learned about several pieces of software that have helped. Two of them are "Endnote" and "Nvivo". Endnote helps with references. You can "cite while you write", which will automatically put the references in the format you choose (APA for example) and place the reference in the bibliography while you are writing. Very cool! You still need to check it, but it really speeds up the writing.

**Monica** recalls that researching the types of technology to use was very time consuming. The best tips were from other doctoral students.

Although **Jim B** completed my doctoral work at a major public research university, there was a lack of campus support for qual data analysis software. I was fortunate that my research team membership provided NVivo. In **Francesca**'s classes, we learned how to code documents. However, they used the old-fashioned method of multi-colored markers and index cards and files. Then we tried it using NVivo – a qual software program. What a difference! It is basically the same procedure, but it saves so much time!

**Roxanne**'s analysis was done using Microsoft Word and Excel. I purchased NVivo and just felt I would rather dive into the data than waste time learning the software. I am not sure whether my decision was a good one, but it does provide evidence that software is not necessary for QR.

**Angela F** utilized NVIVO in my data management and analysis but looking back did so inefficiently. **Ellie** was not familiar with new technology in qual data analysis and recognized a lack of technology support.

---

*My colleague at Castleton,* Anne Slonaker, *is very excited about an interview for an oral history she just completed. She used a piece of technology called a* Livescribe *pen, which together with the "dot" paper that accompanies it, provides the user with both textual and voice reference points. Check out* http://www. livescribe.com. *This technology is way cool! Thanks, Anne! A former dean and dear friend,* Joan Mulligan, *also just showed me how to speak into the Iphone and have my words automatically typed out! (yes, I live in rural, less-wired, Vermont!) I could imagine getting my thoughts down while driving back from my interviews as opposed to talking into a tape recorder and transcribing them later. Technology is one area that is clearly transforming aspects of the QR process and will make this section of the book "old". Please update your own knowledge in this area in order to help yourself succeed.*

## TIME

**Tiffany** could have finished my dissertation much faster if I had used quant methods. I had originally sketched out a quant dissertation study with my advisor; I would have completed data collection within 10 weeks. Although sound, the study simply didn't excite me. It didn't "feel" right. I couldn't envision myself owning it. When I started to draft the qual proposal, it sort of flowed out of me, and I was passionate about it. So, although it took me 2 years to complete my dissertation, I had enough interest and enthusiasm about it to keep me going.

**Jim O** was not prepared for the amount of time the data analysis process would require. I remember saying to my chair at one point, "*Why* didn't I just go quant like my other cohort members?" In hindsight, I recognize and am thankful that I stuck with a qual approach as it enabled me to gain a much deeper understanding of my participants and also my topic.

It took time to follow up with each member of the focus group and for those females that agreed to longer individual interviews. However, it helped in protecting the validity of **Tom**'s work.

A QS takes time in the field doing observations and interviews, as well as time on your own transcribing and analyzing. Make sure you *really* like the topic! **Michelle** is excited to learn whenever I observe or do an interview. What I am seeing and hearing is truly fascinating to me, causing me to ask more questions and confirm thoughts I may have already had.

During the whole course and dissertation period **Mary** worked full time, so the time frame to completion expanded to almost a year longer than I expected. In addition, materials had to be submitted and signed off by library and various levels almost a semester before actual graduation; that extended time, too. I did finish everything in 7 years from when I began the first course. I am still proud of that.

## SURPRISES?

**Brighid** (*italics that follow are hers*): *Make sure you know what you are getting into!* QR is intense. It can take a *really* long time. You never really know what challenges you might encounter so *prepare for the unexpected.* Life does not stand still while you are in graduate school. You can't always predict what family emergencies might happen that can impact your data collection and research process. I had two children while completing my dissertation. I expected to get a lot of work completed while pregnant, but it didn't happen. When you essentially have a nine-month stomach flu, there is not a lot of any type of work that can be completed.

**Jim O** was surprised to find out that one of my participants, a lesbian, had been date raped by a young man, which had a profound impact on her life and how she now relates to males her own age. I was more surprised when the other female participants knew about the issue and had multiple friends who had been raped. These stories and the pain conveyed through them really opened my eyes, making me seriously question if I could convey the information to my readers. To make sure that I adequately told this part of her story and also that I didn't share too much personal information, I asked the young woman to assist me in writing that section of my dissertation.

**Nancy**'s committee chair was the qual statistics instructor and very supportive. Another member of my committee, also very supportive, passed away mid-way through my program; I had to find another faculty member to take his place (not an easy sell!). The committee asked me to include quant\ instruments in my methodology; it became a mixed methods study at that time. I had to add a pre-screening protocol, an experience survey, a demographics instrument and a satisfaction survey using a Likert scale. Overall, I felt that my support was limited, that their preference would have been I do a quant study. It was discouraging at times.

CONCLUSION

The correspondents have shared some stories of what has happened to them in their departments and universities along the road to completing a qualitative dissertation. Time and technology, for example, seem to work together to support – or thwart – one's sense of success. And, perhaps the one major lesson from 'data analysis, continued' is that we each have to – and you will, too – figure out what it is we are doing. No book – not even this one – can do that work for you. The correspondents and I believe, however, that we can support your capacity for doing so more ably.

DECISIONS, DECISIONS, DECISIONS: CONCLUSION

The correspondents' thinking and doing ought to bring comfort in several ways. Firstly, others have gone through the process; a novice can learn from their experiencing. One piece of knowledge you may have gained is that some things are *not* in your control. As I write this, I think of the word "patience", which became a mantra for me during my own initial learning. It remains with me in the whole of my life, as professor, advisor, colleague, and friend. A second piece of learning the correspondents have foreshadowed is just how much support there is out there for learning and completing QR; they will describe it in more depth in Section Three. Given this fact, I have decided to conclude the look at issues with a letter that could also introduce this next section. **Jodi** Fisler sent "Tips", below, which are "some thoughts on my experience, in no particular order." Concise advice seems a fitting conclusion to Section Two, which has focused on issues and obstacles across the range of experiences when learning by doing.

1. There is no one right way to do non-positivistic QR. I was raised to think scientifically; I take comfort in standardized procedures when I am doing something new. Even if you use an interview guide, non-positivistic interviews can only be but so uniform. Different researchers would ask different follow-up questions and arrive at different interpretations, and that's okay. The rigor comes from the care you take to ensure that the data are sound and your interpretations are reasonable and defensible, as opposed to correct.

2. Maintaining neutrality is a nice idea, but the decision about what to tell participants about our reasons for being interested in our research is a little complex. I was told to be very vague about my motivations for doing the study, and certainly about my own ideological perspective, until the study was finished. The reason given was that the data could be compromised if people were reacting to me instead of just responding honestly to the questions. But really, when aren't they reacting and responding to the researcher? If they like you or don't like you, that will affect how they respond to your questions. If you ask a question that takes them down one path mentally or emotionally, their other responses will probably be affected by that. I had several instances where I thought being vague might have actually hindered people's openness, and other instances where I suspected that their assumptions about my ideology were causing them to speak more freely than they might have otherwise. I am also sure that an astute observer would have been able to figure out where I was coming from by the assumptions implicit in my questions. The best thing is to be honest with yourself; notice when your own perspective is coming into play. Keeping a journal is a great way to process some of those observations.

3. Keep a journal! It was helpful, not to mention interesting, to be able to go back and see what I was thinking after early interviews and to be able to trace the development of my analysis. It was a useful tool for working through my own reactions to the participants and my observations about the process itself. It was hard to make time for it sometimes, but it really was worth it!

4. Analyze as you go along. I got a little too far ahead of myself with interviewing and realized later that I had missed some good avenues for follow-up with some participants. Fortunately, I had communicated with my advisor about what I was doing. She suggested I should hold off on any further interviews until I could catch up with the analysis. Good advice. I had regarded the interview part as a distinct phase I wanted to get through in order to feel like I was making progress. Ideally, all of the pieces of the process move forward together, more or less, even though it didn't feel as satisfying as being able to check off "Finish interviews" on my to-do list.

5. Everything took longer than I anticipated. IRB approval took forever. Each aspect—interviews, transcribing, coding, writing—demanded a lot more time than what I had planned. I think you just can't rush intellectual work. Ideas germinate and mature on their own schedule.

6. Aside from that, I found that taking time away to rejuvenate, spend quality time with family, or to work on household projects was very helpful. That's part of the reason things took longer, but I think I was a happier, nicer, and saner person for it in the end.

7. Sleep is key. Sleeping on a problem can help you work through it. My advisor talked about giving myself time and space to sit with my questions and let answers, ideas, etc bubble up from within. The control freak in me wanted to have things happen on a certain schedule, but sometimes the best way to grapple with a tough section of analysis was to wrestle with it for a while and then sleep on it for a few days. At a certain point, you need to let go and trust yourself and the process to work.

8. Remember that interviewing is an art as well as a skill. Even after 40+ interviews, I still cringed at times when I was reviewing the recordings. I found it difficult to maintain the right balance between being in "researcher mode" and being more open and conversational, which is my way of being friendly. The phrasing of my follow-up questions got better over the course of the study, but still wasn't as good as I would have liked.

# FACETS OF SUPPORT

**Carin:** We learned from one another. I cannot put a price tag on the value of my dissertation study group or our chair who was there with us each step of the way.

## INTRODUCTION

The largest category of support for undertaking QR for a master's thesis or dissertation is that of other human beings, whether they be faculty members on or off committee and colleagues/peers going through the same thing. When you read the reflections of the correspondents writing here, you will get a sense that talking with someone(s) who gets it – and gets you – is crucial to one's well-being. Additionally, although "family support" is not given a heading in this section, I think you will find it to be indispensable, as several letters in the remaining pages of the book will make painfully clear. You may recall Crystal's story about choosing to explore her younger brother's experiences, out of love, an idea that had her family "being on board" (p. 42). Descriptions of finishing a work of QR are often coupled with an awareness if not an explicit acknowledgement of loved ones. Sometimes, it seems we forget these people when so much of the work feels like it is ours, alone (e.g., Karen H, p. 110). In this space, then, I ask you *not* to forget the love in your life while you work like crazy to complete your qualitative research. Even if you feel like you are alone, let the correspondents who are here – and who wrote in caring ways so you would not be alone – be your loving, supportive, and respectful companions. This care for self and others, matters.

QUESTION FOUR: WHAT SUPPORTS FOR QR EXIST AT YOUR UNIVERSITY?

**Monica** *suggests:* If you are doing research on the student-athlete population, you can provide compensation as long as it is approved in your IRB. Think out the incentives or rewards you want to give to your participants ahead of time. The bylaw is out of the NCAA Manual Bylaw 16.11.1.11.1 Institution-Based Research Studies. Also make sure you check in and get the approval of the Athletics Compliance Office of the Institution. I know about this topic, because I had to go back and add in my compensation!

## BUILDING A COMMITTEE

**Donna** always felt as if I had enormous support. One of my committee members was a devout "Quantie" and proud of that label! I chose her to provide a balanced voice. I felt if she could understand and appreciate the research, then I had succeeded in reaching a varied audience.

Selecting the right chair and committee who have an interest in QR is important. Within **Jessie**'s program, our chair must be within our area of specialization. Beyond that, I tried to diversify my committee to bring to the table a variety of perspectives about my work and methods, even one who specializes in quant studies so that I can understand how someone from that frame of reference might view my work.

**Vic**'s qual course professor was my committee chairperson. Three of my five committee members also had experience in QR. I can see how it would be a challenge if the majority of your committee was not ambidextrous.

> *Two different voices, below, describe some of the difficulties you could encounter when building your committee.*

**ANON** In our program, the student essentially inherits the committee members. I realized that would not work in my case. It was a politically charged decision to go to my advisor and say, "This won't work; it won't ever get completed." The relationship of trust and mutual respect between advisor and student allowed me to request a committee "outside the tradition" and offer a valid and logical argument as to why this was in everyone's best interest. My advisor took the heat for this decision and protected me.

**ANON** Finding members for my dissertation committee who are supportive of a QD was a bit tricky. My advisor gave me a rather short list of possibilities; we found great people who are okay with my methodology and the emergent nature of my study.

**Tom** *asserts that* developing a good relationship with each member and keeping them up to date at all times is important. Most have other responsibilities. I spent much of my early program meeting professors and reaching out to others within the department that I did not have for class in order to build a strong committee.

Despite doing this pre-committee groundwork, be prepared for questions that may make you feel dejected. At one point, I believed my gender would be an issue for one committee member. She wasn't sure that as a male, I could fully understand a female's perspectives, which is true to a point, but I addressed this in my study by stating:

A critical postmodern feminist critique by some would state that as a male, I could not fully understand or appreciate a female perspective. However, the participants did not shy away from discussing gender bias or discrimination. In fact, many of them seemed to open up on the topic in the focus group discussions. Having familiarity or a prior relationship with a researcher can help interviewees to be comfortable in sharing their story (Bogden & Biklen, 2003). p. 114 (*lightly edited*)

**ANON** Know the load of your dissertation chair. Don't pick a chair with 15 advisees or someone who is chairing 10 committees, especially if the students are all in the same phase of the process. Also, if your chair is a department head or has a lot of other responsibilities, he/she is not going tob e able to get back to you quickly.

**Cindy** cannot stress enough how important the dissertation committee is. I found it necessary to start thinking about who I wanted two years before I asked the question of potential committee members. It was important to understand the committee member beyond his/her level of knowledge on the subject. ADVICE: You must understand how committed s/he is to your research, how quickly s/he will respond to communication, the types of contacts and resources the person has, etc. Again, my decision was calculated and required intensive research. The investment was worth it. My advisor was a key to my success. He navigated the waters when they were rocky.

Additionally, three of the four committee members were willing to read every chapter in order to offer suggestions and question my rationale. The writing and re-writing was one of the best experiences of the dissertation process. I learned more than any course could teach me. Appreciate the gift your committee/advisor offers – the gift of time, which is priceless.

**Veronica** *reports that* although having two advisors, one for methodology and one for content, can be challenging because of different philosophies and overall focus, the support I received was amazing. I felt empowered to go outside of the norm not only in terms of methodology (I developed a new methodology focused on context, which drew on four established qualitative methodologies) but also in terms of exploring a topic (content area literacy) with innovative methods (e.g., photo-elicitation interviewing and retrospective think-aloud interviewing). My advisors both provided insight, knowledge, and questions in their respective areas of expertise, moving me into new areas of growth and independence.

Their support also crossed into my personal life. Being in a doctoral program was the most taxing experience of my life. At times, the educational process of teaching, learning, and researching overwhelmed me. At other times my life outside of school took over. No matter which plunging wave consumed me, my advisors were always there to listen, giving me the space to sit with the not knowing, to sit with the tension of my life, to sit with my tears. Then they would say exactly what I needed to hear whether it was advice, affirmation, or a question.

*As **Hilary** suggests below, she could have been better prepared for the life-changing experience doing her research was. You may conclude at some point during this* *section/by the end of the book that sometimes we get in our own way, partly because of what we do not yet know and partly, simply because of who we are and how we handle things – or not.*

*Amplifying the Text*: Hilary Levey Friedman

Dear Judith,

Writing my qualitative dissertation **was a life-changing experience**—not only because of its academic and professional implications, but also for its personal ones. I want to highlight some of the ways in which I personally was affected by my qualitative research experiences. I think we still do not discuss these issues often enough or openly enough in the academy. I do think this is changing somewhat with respect to romantic entanglements in the field, but I think personal impacts are completely overlooked or not taken seriously.

From June 2006 to September 2007 I immersed myself in the worlds of competitive afterschool activities. Specifically, I studied families with elementary school-age children who participate in chess, dance, or soccer. I joke it was like I had kids, but I don't, because I spent nights and weekends on athletic fields, in dance studios, at community spaces, and in hotel ballrooms. I put 10,000 miles on my car as I traveled to practices and competitive events (like state and national tournaments) and to interview 172 people (95 parents, some of their children, and teachers and coaches). It is not at all inaccurate to say I gave my life over to this project.

And, I really did. Studying parents, and their hopes and dreams for their own children, helped crystallize my own hopes and dreams and what I wanted out of life. During this time I ended a serious romantic relationship and let friendships drift. These decisions where obviously related to issues and struggles before I began fieldwork, but the work on my particular topic and the act of meeting new people and seeing how families lived was a serious impetus in my own life changes.

But I also made new friends, sometimes among those I met while doing fieldwork. Today I am still Facebook friends with some of them, I exchange holiday cards and emails with others, and I even invited two to my recent wedding. When three families attended my dissertation defense and celebration with their kids, my advisors remarked that they had never seen this happen before. To me, it was only natural given the closeness I felt to some of the families.

Because I hung out so much in these environments and had deep conversations about raising kids (which obviously included fears about the future), I felt like sometimes I was part therapist. Parents confessed to me when they worried a child might be gay, when they worried about the effects of a divorce on their child, and when they worried they were making their child dysfunctional. Often, they turned to me for advice and clarification. While I offered it the best I could, I confess when I drove home at night I sometimes cried, wondering if I would ever "figure it out" for myself. I, foolishly, had always thought parents "had it together" when they had kids, and clearly that wasn't true. How could I think about a family someday if I still didn't know what I wanted to be "when I grew up?" This research made me question my future goals, but in the end, it also helped clarify them.

Doing this work made me a better researcher, thinker, scholar, and person. I can't imagine doing an extensive project like this again all by myself though (again, for personal and practical reasons). I don't think advisors prepare students for the fact that doing research like this can change you as a person, and that is a fault that should be remedied… someday "when I grow up" maybe? Sincerely, Hilary

## COMMITTEE AND FINANCIAL SUPPORT

Find a chair and committee members who are supportive! **Monica**'s chair's area of expertise is not exactly what my dissertation covers, but having someone who is in my corner goes farther sometimes. Although you may have some idea of who you would like to have on your committee, ask your chair to suggest members, and check with him/her about any ideas you may have. Having a committee who gets along can make your path smoother.

Luckily, **Jim O**'s advisor and the other members of my DC were knowledgeable and experienced in QR and were helpful in guiding me through the process.

Both co-chairs of **Joan**'s committee are qual researchers; several faculty members, including **Bruce**'s chair, are qual researchers.

At the time **Lisa W** was working on my QD, my chair and at least one of my committee members were involved heavily in QR. Many faculty members in my department and College knew about QR and shared the dilemmas, road blocks and issues they had faced.

**Angela F**'s advisor and one professor on my committee, who was not in my department, were with me through the whole process. My department itself went through many changes while I was in this process, which led to lot of turnover; there was one professor in another department who really provided the longevity in support I needed as a developing scholar.

**ANON** did not have a QM person on the committee. In fact, one member was very opposed to the kind of study I described as well as my efforts to synthesize several conceptual models. None of this came out until chapter reviews; there had been no push back during the proposal stage. A supportive chair declared that if it was approved in the proposal, then I should be able to carry it out that way. He offered to change that person, but I decided it was important for me to work it out, and we did. It was not fun, but I felt stronger for doing so.

**Francesca**'s committee had no experience with Policy Discourse Analysis (PDA) (Ball, 2006; Glynos, Howarth, Norval & Speed, 2009) as a method. I had to clearly and carefully define and explain why this was the best method to answer my research question. They were not opposed to QM at all; it was more a matter of them not knowing specifically about PDA and needing more information. My advisor was solidly behind my choice.

Our faculty also encourages students to submit papers to conferences. They also bring alumni back to explain their research to us and why they chose qual or quant as a methodology. The computer lab has several QR programs for our use.

Financial support was essential. **Angela F** had fellowships, graduate assistantships and outside internships and research jobs. The support of the Spencer Foundation's research and travel program was there for me.

**Kristan** was affiliated with the Center for Higher Education Policy analysis as a research associate and the Center for American Studies and Ethnicity as a Minority Doctoral Ford Fellow; both centers provided direct support for developing my qual project, particularly from my advisor and peers. I was also in the inaugural class of ASHE/Lumina Fellows.

**Sandy** did receive a financial award from an alumni group to help finance my travel. My chair and other committee members and departmental faculty were familiar with and accomplished in QR and supportive of my work. They provided examples of previous work that I used to help organize my research and my writing. I was also able to access ATLASti from the university to assist in the analysis of my interview transcriptions. RefWorks helped to organize references.

**Mary** *reported that* the Graduate School of Education (GSE) provides some travel support so students can attend national conferences.

## GENERAL SUPPORT

**Ginny** believes my institution has some of the best qual researchers around. They are very understanding of the sometimes uncomfortable nature of drawing conclusions compared to a quant study. **Corey** could not have asked for a better place to be.

**ANON** is thankful that both of my doctoral programs (I transferred) supported my decision to take both qual and quant research methods classes. The faculty helped me build my understanding of QR through collaborations on multiple projects. However, I didn't feel that I had a lot of people with whom I could discuss troubles with data analysis, sampling, etc. I felt a little stuck; less senior graduate students came to me to ask these questions, which I answered to the best of my ability, and faculty offered pats on the back, but many in my immediate vicinity weren't able to offer real methodological advice in this area.

**ANON** There wasn't a lot of support for QR at my university outside of the dissertation committee and my advisor. The college had software and labs for quant research but not for QR.

## DEPARTMENT SUPPORT

**ANON**'s department is largely comprised of qual research faculty. My impression is that they are largely unavailable. My committee is very "hands off" in many ways…I don't want to knock them because they have been helpful in providing practical advice to keep me going forward, but any 'extra' I need to look for elsewhere. My understanding of QR has come from reading books, journal articles, and I also belong to a listserv (Qualrs-L Qualitative Research for the Human Sciences).

**ANON**'s whole world was my department. I did not rely on alumni, or conferences, or even internet connections. I was completely dependent upon the faculty and some of my colleagues to help me through the process; there was no Facebook, My Space, or forum that I connected with to aid in my process.

There was little departmental support available for QR; (**ANON**'s) doctoral program only provided one course on QR, and the scope and depth of it were superficial.

## COHORT/ALUMNI/PEER SUPPORT

**Ronn** found that my cohort and recent graduates were essential. A few members of my cohort provided emotional support and encouragement as we all moved through the process together. We met once a month to discuss the process and offer each other ideas. Also, a graduate of our program agreed to work with me. She had had the same dissertation chair. She read a draft of each chapter, provided advice, caught errors, and wrote comments about issues my chair might raise.

The alumni who helped **Mary** were members of my incoming group who preceded me by a year in graduation; they had lots of hints and support.

**Kristan** attended a two week preparation seminar to develop my proposal. One of the highlights was being with individuals who were from different disciplines. I got feedback from varying perspectives, which strengthened my proposal and how I thought about doing my work.

### *Dissertation Study Groups (DSG)*

**Carin**'s DSG was the group of peers I "lived with" for three plus years. I joined before completing my coursework, eager to learn about the process. All members had the same chair; we connected because we were using a similar research approach. The DSG met every two weeks. At each meeting members gave an update on their progress, areas of significant learning, and, later on, their findings.

I decided I wanted to write something for each meeting; my goal was to send it to my chair prior to so that he could provide feedback at the meeting. Each time I gave him something, he had read it and gave feedback at the meeting. Perhaps he was able to do so because not everyone submitted materials for each meeting. I am fortunate that I had a chair who was always timely in providing feedback. A few pages each week adds up; this self-imposed deadline worked to my advantage.

**Anabella** felt most comfortable and actually safe to talk about QR in the context of a dissertation seminar with my sponsor and other students who were also undertaking research on topics related to teaching and learning in higher education. I did not feel I needed to justify myself or my interest in undertaking QR.

As a group member, I experienced some of the characteristics of what Wenger (1998) defines as a community of practice. All members were at different stages of their program, so we were able to learn from each other certain strategies and approaches that were necessary in order to complete the tasks required of the different phases of the dissertation process. Our interactions created a "shared repertoire" (Wenger, 1998) of experiences, approaches and understandings of QR. I think it was this group, our debates, and our mutually constructed understanding of QR that constituted the most significant source of support for undertaking my QR dissertation.

Several students in **Sandy**'s cohort established a writing group to provide support and motivation. We were all using QM, so we were able to be a resource for each other.

**Isabelle** received a lot of help and support from my fellow students. We had a bi-weekly discussion group; I would not have found a solution to my dilemma – how to interview without giving my nationality away – without their help. Bottom line, talking and talking about my research design with those who were going through similar issues helped tremendously. They had a different perspective than mine, were not involved with the topic and thus they were able to critique and ask questions that made me reflect and rethink the process constantly.

## LITERATURE REVIEW/SUPPORT FROM AUTHORS/RESEARCHERS

**Tom** found many researchers that were still active in the field when conducting my LR. I used the internet to find email addresses to contact some of these men and women. These individuals proved to be an invaluable resource; a good number of them returned my email and gave me some insights of what to avoid and look out for when doing my study. One of the big things was to make sure that you practice interviewing skills. You have your guiding questions to get the conversation started but then you have to be ready with probing questions and also at the same time keep the participant comfortable.

### Books

One book stands out both because of its quality but also because of a key point in the process for **Angela F**. It is Potter's (1996) book *An Analysis of Thinking and Research about Qualitative Methods*. My advisor recommended it when I was taking the daunting steps to admit that I was a constructivist, and that I wanted to develop a method for the work rather than adopt an existing QM. This particular book helped me to understand the essence of qual concepts at such a deep level that I could pursue my ambitions and fully embrace my potential.

In choosing **Jessie**'s methodology, case study seemed a natural, as the participants were bound by a shared experience; ethnography was another option, viewing the groups of student volunteers as a culture. Both left me thinking the study would remain lacking. In the advanced qual course, I read *Narrative Learning* (Goodson, Biesta, Teddar, and Adair, 2010) that was absolutely inspiring and provided a framework.

**Amanda**'s qual methodologist encouraged me to press the envelope. He suggested I read *Qualitative Research Design* (Maxwell, 2005). This book opened my thinking and made me feel free. I learned that I became too free, however, and had to be brought back to some type of structure so that the quality of my work was evident and did not seem haphazard.

## CONFERENCES

**Donna** began to attend conferences that supported QM, such as the Society of Philosophy and History of Education (SOPHE) and the American Educational Studies Association (AESA). In those conferences, a brand new world of support opened for me.

## FACULTY SUPPORT

**ANON** There are two wonderful qual professors in my program. If it wasn't for them, I would have left after getting my master's; thankfully, one is my advisor.

**Katherine** was blessed with great faculty who were quite open to crafting coursework that was designed especially for me and my interests. I took many independent studies with extensive reading lists. These were incredibly important to my development as a researcher!

*Once again, I choose to break away from the reporting of external supports to provide another whole story lest you think getting this work done and done well is a matter of being in the right place at the right time with the right people, which OF COURSE is a wonderful thing, but we all know the aphorism: wherever you go, there you are. I thank* **Karen H** *for her brave letter.*

*Amplifying the Text*: Karen Hammel (*slightly abbreviated*)

I always thought of qualitative data as the softer side of research, representing real people in real situations. The data, I assumed, would be harder to collect (human subjects) but easier to analyze (no definitive answers or clear implications). I never actually got a chance to choose QR; it chose me. This is my story.

Arrogant and sarcastic, I did not endear myself to the faculty of the college of education. Called to the office of the dean for disrespecting a junior professor, I was irreverent and unapologetic. I did not realize that I was a breath away from being dismissed from the doctoral program. A miracle came in the form of an *experiential simulation* and its creator, Dr. C. Cryss Brunner (2003). Designed to strip away identity and confront assumptions about leadership, ourselves and others, the on-line exercise changed my life. Within the simulation, I was left empty handed and alone with my arrogance and sarcasm.

I thought I was a leader in education, but (aside from force) I didn't even know what leadership was. Suddenly, I wasn't even sure who I was. The research questions and design flowed from that deeply personal, deeply humiliating experience....

Self study is both radical and presumptuous. While Dr. Brunner's sponsorship saved me from dismissal, my committee was not in full support of my study. Some members questioned the place of potentially traumatic personal transformation in academia. One member excused herself. Were it not for Dr. Brunner, as advisor, ally and mentor, the study would not have been done. Perhaps I would still have changed, perhaps not. Either way, the lessons I learned would not have been captured, studied and passed along.

Asserting that would-be leaders must consider the nature of the self or being, the purpose of the study was to come to understand and document the phenomenon of personal transformation—in particular, parts of the transformation related to notions of leadership, power and identity. Phenomenological methods, including journaling, professional documents, and purposeful reading, were used to document the personal experience of change. Ethnographic methods, including ongoing mentoring, 100+ surveys, 22 phenomenological interviews and interpersonal anecdotes, explored the social and interconnected aspects of such a change. Critical theory, existentialism and neo-Marxism provided the lens of interpretation.

The conclusions and implications were intended to capture the essence of the experience, articulate lessons learned, and construct an individual model of transformation. The final product, deeply personal yet broadly resonant, covered seven years, crossed five school districts and generated more than one thousand data points. Although radical in many ways, the five hundred page dissertation followed a traditional format. ...

Reflecting on the process, I am struck by the loneliness of it all; no one can do it for you or with you. As an intellectual and scholar, I knew that an enduring and insightful study was more important than walking across the stage. Although there were times I thought about "divorce", I have no regrets. I needed my diverse and cautious committee; my design was custom tailored not for ease, but for depth and impact. To divorce my topic, I would have had to give up on myself as leader, scholar and authentic individual.

The lesson I would most like to pass on to anyone undertaking QR is: put *yourself* into the study. This is not to say that everyone should study themselves. QR offers the unique opportunity to engage with your study in personal ways. Choose a topic that ignites passion and drives the imagination. Make the study meaningful to you so it can be meaningful to others. Stay married to it long after the dissertation is done. Thanks, Judy. Sincerely, Karen

### FACULTY SUPPORT (CONTINUED)

Faculty were excellent guides, but **Isabelle** had to ask the right questions; the more specific I was, the more help I received. You cannot be vague; you have to know exactly what you are looking for, and you will receive adequate direction.

The support of a mentor has been invaluable! **Michelle**'s advisor has guided me step by step, yet has allowed me the room to grow and build confidence in my abilities as a researcher. She has given me the tools I need and allowed me the freedom use those tools to fit my research. I draw on her expertise when I have questions, and she provides a peer review of my work that can facilitate discussions on areas I may not have thought of or noticed.

Lots of support exists in **Amanda**'s program. All faculty members support new and innovative research methods that make positive contributions to the identified gap the current research study intends to fill. A new qual researcher came on board, and my chair was enthusiastic about him joining our project. Most importantly, the researcher who espoused meta-interpretation communicated with me via email and shared personal experiences during the entire process of my dissertation research.

At **Jim B**'s doctoral institution, there were a number of very supportive faculty members who engaged in QR themselves, taught QM courses, and invited students to work on QR with them. I had the great luck to study with three such faculty members.

**Anabella** was mentored by QR faculty who are positioned in the field. It was crucial for me to "see" how respected scholars were following a QR approach and contributing significantly to the literature. This opportunity included working with them on papers to present at conferences.

**Tiffany** had a brilliant qual researcher who taught advanced coursework. Although she was not my advisor, she served as almost a second advisor to any student who needed her help.

**Vic** relied heavily on my chairperson to assist me. We meet every week to two weeks for a period of about three months to get a handle on content, in terms of salient themes and categories, and how to present the findings. Not until late in the analysis process did the resolution to this last issue reveal itself. In hindsight, I now realize that the type of report should be dependent upon the data and analysis rather than any preconceived notions. We as students tend to want structure and direction.

**Cassandra** must emphasize the importance of having not only a compatible chair but also a methodologist to work with. As a result of my efforts and thoroughness to carefully locate the most appropriate study population, my methodologist realized I was serious about conducting my study. From that point on, she was my biggest champion for ensuring I did the best job I could.

When **Mary** had a last conference with my chair before the defense, he said I should expect a strong challenge from the other committee member on QM, synthesis ideas, and related questions about the value of my work. I prepared for these questions and apparently my little speech about the values and methods of qual and quant research and rigor was effective when – surprise to me – my chair asked those questions, just another example of the strong support I received from him.

> *"Faculty support" is one area of major change since the 1980s, which makes my heart sing and serves education proudly. True, there are places and persons who support QR more or less as they did 30 years ago, but there are many more persons and places that now encourage, challenge, and guide undergraduate, masters', and doctoral students along this path. Finding these individuals at your university is easier than ever before. Remember, too, they may be hidden in plain sight; we just hired an associate dean,* Yasmine Ziesler, *who is an anthropologist! I finally have someone to talk with here who "gets it"!*

## LIBRARY SUPPORT

**Mary** *praises* the library and librarians as a HUGE help. Toward the end, the person who supervised and passed on the format for submission was extremely kind and helpful, creating templates for us to use. Our library has great internet access, full text data bases, and access to… other more distant libraries. It seemed like magic to be able to request things and have them appear a few days later! The library also sponsored one small tutorial for qual software.

**Cindy** *suggests* that librarians have special skills and can find unknown studies for your LR that might not readily appear in your initial database searches.

## WORKING FROM A SATELLITE CAMPUS

**Julie** *raves:* QR faculty are very supportive! I am in a unique situation where I have attended all of my classes at a satellite campus of GW. While we have some full-time faculty on staff, most are located up in DC – so support is available, but not very hands on.

*I think* Hilary *was right earlier in this section when she writes about the life-changing impact of choosing this work and the lack of emphasis IHEs place on that likelihood and perhaps, inevitability. In this section I chose to insert three "whole" reflections as "interruptions" among the briefer segments because I wanted to remind you, more than once, that the correspondents – my data set – are thoughtful and caring individuals, whom you are able to get a truer sense of from their whole thoughts to you. Each author addresses what it was "really" like to be "in my shoes"; they connect their experiencing to their deliberation and actions.* Hilary *made it through, in part with the support of her participants; both* Karen H *and* **Angela LV**, *below, had someone who cared enough to help them. We all want you to remember you are a* real *person doing* real *work in a complex,* real *world. Remember, too, that English is* **not** Angela LV's *native language! Be awed! Be aware! And as we conclude Section III, know we urge you to please take care!*

### *Concluding Section Three*: Angela Lopez-Velasquez

The multiple pressures involved in producing a dissertation that will grant a doctoral degree often result in Ph.D. students encountering emotional struggles during their dissertation writing time. Few talk about these struggles for fear of being perceived as weak or inadequate. In consequence, many Ph.D. students face emotional difficulties alone, or drop their dream of getting their degree. I struggled with anxiety and depression during my dissertation writing time. Although hard, this experience has become one of the major learning experiences of my life, and one that I often share with friends who are going through something similar during their dissertation writing. As a highly socially-oriented person, and perceived by friends and family as a happy-go-lucky, motivated, and excited human being, it was difficult for me to realize that I was struggling with depression, and even harder for others to understand that I could possibly be affected by an emotional disorder. So little did I know of anxiety and depression that it took someone else to point it out for me. A life-time overachiever, I was always hard on myself; I thought that the difficulties I was facing making progress on the dissertation were due to my own incapability of managing my work and time, and not due to other elements outside of my control.

After 5 years of not seeing each other, my sister came to the US for a visit during Christmas break. She must have seen the distress that I was going through, and how such distress has changed my main personality traits. She noticed that I was much less active and that I have lost interest in the activities that otherwise would excite me. She also noticed that I was often tired and easily irritable, and that even a simple task will appear overwhelming to me. In our sister-to-sister conversations, I admitted to her that it was hard for me to focus and that even reading had become a daunting activity, as I could not hold my concentration for more than a couple of sentences at a time. Something was wrong with me. I had taken notice, but not given it much importance simply because I did not have the "time" to figure out what was going on. "I have to finish this dissertation!" was my argument for not doing anything else that would require extra thinking from my part. Driven by the huge responsibility of finishing the program and getting my degree, I pushed through the debilitating feelings, thinking that I could not have the luxury of taking time off the dissertation to figure out my personal issues. As a result of the untreated condition, and regardless of how much daily time I dedicated to writing, I made little progress, which in turn made me more overwhelmed and anxious. I did not know that every day I was digging myself deeper and deeper into the depression.

With my sister's help, I started considering that I needed to reach out for help. I made an appointment with a counselor, who was a great listener and had experience with women and depression. With her, I was able to figure out that I was experiencing something that I could not control, and that I needed help to deal with it. I started learning more about emotional disorders and realized that mental health is often a neglected part of our education. The therapy sessions helped me to give myself permission to take breaks from the dissertation to explore what I was going through, and to find a solution. I first struggled with the idea of a treatment that involved medicines, but eventually I accepted the need for them and started taking the prescribed pills. A clear feeling of relief came after a couple of weeks into the treatment, and I slowly regained the capacity to focus my attention, to feel motivated and excited even about the dissertation. Taking care of the depression helped me finish my dissertation successfully. I am grateful for the support that I found in my sister and in the professional help I received.

Most people who enroll in a Ph.D. program are aware of the academic demands of getting a doctoral degree, and sign up for it with a consciousness of the intellectual efforts they will have to make. Few, however, know of the fact that years of dedicated study – and for many of combining study and work – will inevitably take a toll on one's emotional well-being, due to the almost obligatory imbalance that one's life has to be submitted to. Living through years with limited time and energy to spend in nurturing connections to family and friends, compounded by the constant feeling of having to tackle a titanic project (as is the dissertation), can easily breed isolation and anxiety. It is of paramount importance that dissertation writers are aware of the challenges and of the possible impact that it could have on their physical and mental health, so that they can take care of themselves and accomplish their goals.

# REFLECTIONS ON METHODOLOGY

**Monica:** People have said that I don't need to love my topic, however, I disagree. Many times when I was discouraged, just rereading what I had done so far renewed my resolve to complete the dissertation. The interviews I have done with my participants have also given me a boost. I am enjoying gathering the data and the whole process of getting through my most difficult academic challenge.

## INTRODUCTION

I ended an earlier draft of Section One with a portion of a letter from **Xyan**. I split her letter into two parts because she wrote specifically about practice *and* theory, with which we begin here. I will continue with Shaunna's discussion of "positionalilty" and contributions from Katherine, Cassie, and Veronica. This opening portion of Section Four concludes by returning yet once more to the thoughts of Shaunna and Wanju about language.

QUESTION FIVE: WHAT METHODOLOGICAL ISSUES DID YOU FACE?

*"…and Theory"* – Xyan Neider

I would like now to turn to the more interesting aspects of my QD, because rather than methods and processes, this part of my reflection focuses on the broader picture – what we have to learn about ourselves as scholars, researchers, and members of the world.

The journey through my QD allowed me to heal "much of my own diseased thinking…through exploration, engagement with my participants, and working to respectfully re/present their stories" (Neider, p. 263). I, too, have been affected by the framings of the Middle East and Muslims as trouble through media, interactions with others, and various other social forces. A postcolonial theoretical framework also helped me to reflect and identify this fact in my own knowledge constructions and explore it in my own work. Writing a QD allowed me to investigate and strengthen how "my way of being within the world, is built upon the legacies of my own family and through…[this]…work, I…[was]…brought closer to them and their love…[was]…realized through me" (p. 263).

Because I chose to explore a contemporary issue, affecting a particular group of students on U.S. college campuses, using a QM, I was able to re/educate myself, close gaps in my own knowledge and learning, and delve more deeply into mechanisms that construct subordination, domination, and oppression. As my study progressed, I came to realize that perhaps the only way to get to the underlying contextual issues I wanted to explore, illuminate, and disrupt was through the use of an inclusive methodology that allowed a greater cohesion with critical epistemologies. My theoretical framework of postcolonial theory, e.g., Appadurai (1993; 1999), Au (2008), Friedman (1992), Hardt & Negri (2000) Meyer (2004), Mohanty (1984), worked in tandem with my methods and opened spaces for me to understand, explore, and theorize about how knowledge is constructed and maintained about identities and spaces within which students interact. Further, postcolonial theory made room for me to unearth my own systems of knowledge construction about members of the group I researched, an inclusivity that isn't honored within quant methods.

At times, the process of constructing a dissertation was arduous. Often, I remember thinking to myself – as I do now – "Wow! I am so glad I have chosen a topic I love and am so grateful that I have chosen to make use of a critical theoretical perspective because it has kept my data fresh, new, fluid, and rich." Postcolonial theory also kept my mind agile, helping me to be cognizant of and responsible to the knowledge I was constructing about a group unlike myself. I kept returning to the questions postcolonial theory generates: whose knowledge is privileged, the purpose of the knowledge, and the consequences of the knowledge, which in turn kept me focused. These questions guided my excavations/immersion into the data and helped me frame my understandings from the data.

As I constructed my first interview questions, I struggled; I wanted inclusive questions that would get to the meaning of the experiences of students of Middle Eastern heritages on a U.S. college campus in a post-9/11 context. I talked with the faculty member who eventually became my dissertation chair. She talked me through aligning the questions I might ask of participants with my overarching goal, exactly like I was teaching my own students at the time. I felt a light bulb turn on in my head: "Yes, my questions needed to align with my purpose/goal! It made sense."

A second insight occurred after course work was finished and my data had been collected. I had hundreds of pages of interview text, observation notes, and academic knowledge. I really struggled with how to begin to analyze my data. I was overwhelmed and kind of stalled trying to figure it out. I wanted to be creative yet didn't quite know how. I didn't want to follow conventional practice in categorizing and classifying my observations and participants, because that flies in the face of postcolonial theory. I also knew I didn't want to write a piece comparing my Middle Eastern students to students in the dominant culture. I wanted to re/present my participants and their stories on their own terms without mythical comparisons that would continue to normalize and neutralize dominance. I regained momentum when my advisor reminded me to incorporate the three questions postcolonial theory generates into my thinking and analysis.

These two insights helped me to find my own process of how to do the work of QI. The second example highlights the importance of using a critical theoretical perspective. In the end, immersion with QM, "a methodology of the heart, a prophetic, feminist postpragmatism that embraces an ethics of truth grounded in love, care, hope and forgiveness", has "the power to heal diseased thinking, damaging narratives, and systematic oppressions" (Denzin, Lincoln, & Giardina, 2006, p. 770). Good luck! Xyan.

**Shaunna**'s Priority Two: Positionality – Know thyself! During my first QR course, I read a book chapter that described the qualitative researcher as *bricoleur*, one who reads widely, is knowledgeable about many interpretive paradigms, thinks in inherently interdisciplinary ways, and understands positionality as part of the research process (Denzin & Lincoln, 2005).

The interpretive *bricoleur* understands that research is an interactive process shaped by his or her own personal history, biography, gender, social class, race, and ethnicity, and by those of the people in the setting. … The political *bricoleur* knows that science is power, for all research findings have political implications. There is no value-free science. (Denzin & Lincoln, 2005, p. 6)

As a blossoming researcher, I exemplified such characteristics. My research topic was formed after reading literature not just from scholarly journals, but from pop culture, biblical texts, theology, and the media such as CNN. Without exaggeration, my positionality – who I was and who I eventually came to be – as a researcher was reflected in my eventual topic of study, the theoretical frameworks used, overall methodology, data analysis, and data presentation. Who I was as a researcher became the backbone of the entire dissertation.

Let me explain. My study was a labor of love. As a result, I had to overcome my own reservations as well as the perceived challenges from my positionality that could have deterred students from participating in my study.

I am a heterosexual, African American, female, and an ordained clergyperson in a historically African American faith tradition that is riddled with homophobia. It was a goal of this study to give particularly thorough attention to ethical human subjects' research and create opportunities to consult with members of nonheterosexual communities who have previously been excluded or marginalized by research processes despite the potential challenges my multiple identities may present. These interests and goals required an understanding of the challenges participants might experience as a result of my exacerbated identities as an "outsider"…. (Payne Gold, 2010, pp. 18 – 19; *edited/jmm*)

I was and still remain an outsider researcher, even as I have extended my line of research within various LGB areas of interest. Yet, I believe that one can (and should) pursue outsider research when one has achieved a level of self-awareness and humility that is required to conceive, craft, and execute such methodology with the help of the communities being studied.

During **Katherine**'s coursework, I was confronted by a few students and professors about conducting cross-cultural research. I was told that I cannot conduct research that concerns students or other participants who are Black, Latina, or any other race besides White. Nor can I do research concerning people who "did not grow up wealthy."

I was devastated. It wasn't until after being immersed in feminist literature and ethnographic works for 2 years that I finally felt "ready" to "defend" my choices. But, instead of coming to the table prepared to "justify" my work to those who might confront me, I instead come prepared to acknowledge that all human beings have both positions of advantage and disadvantage. And, I share my belief that, while it is helpful to "position the author," I do not believe it is fruitful to entertain a contest of marginalities to prove one's academic legitimacy.

A few have criticized my decision to NOT take a critical feminist stance while investigating single-sex public schools. For them, the segregation of the sexes is always wrong, regardless of the context. Some of my Anglo sisters seem to reject my decision to approach the study as a "partner." My Latina and African American colleagues seem to "get" what I am doing/trying to do. I have been told by a few that my desire to *understand* rather than criticize a community's decisions is appreciated.

For me, these conversations really bring to the fore the "problem" with radical feminism: some of us only see gender but do not take into account the importance of intersectionalities, i.e., how race and socio-economic status are important considerations in our research, and our epistemological and philosophical choices. In my case, the community was so desperate to help Latina and African American girls living in poverty, they jumped on the chance to send their daughters to a single-sex public school. They just weren't in a position of privilege to take a philosophical stance against segregation of the sexes. I think that is hard for some of my Anglo feminist sisters to grasp.

***Joining the Text:*** *"Context as a Dissertation Study" –* **Cassie** Quigley
*(abridged, titled)*

When I was in the early stages of my graduate degree, my dissertation loomed in the distant shadows as many professors asked me about my research interests, methodological tendencies, and research questions. As it drew nearer, I constantly worried about where I would conduct my study. I am mother of two young sons (ages 4 and 2 at the time of my dissertation) and a wife of an extremely understanding husband, but I like to control things. I did not want to conduct research away from my family. However, I did not realize that I would design a study around a particular place instead of designing a study and then finding a place to conduct it. That all changed when I walked into the Frankie Woods Science Academy for Girls (FWSAG) located in Gary, Indiana, located just over 200 miles from my home and family. Upon first entering this place, I knew there was something special here. Maybe it was the way the building was painted.... Maybe it was the proud words hanging on the windows declaring, "We Made AYP!" Maybe it was the way parents and community members volunteered. Maybe it was due to my role as a researcher – an outsider invited in to document their story. Regardless of the reason, as I reflect on this decision, I realize that there was a story to be told – one full of goodness and hope in an area that rarely receives this kind of attention. For that reason, I was very deliberate in describing how I entered this school and how this context not only framed my study but was my study.

*I pick up* **Cassie***'s letter where she describes herself related to the context:*

There is a buzzer out front but because this is not my first visit to the school, I know its response will go unanswered, so I pull the door open. This is how I enter Gary: sometimes with a group of researchers, sometimes alone but the path remains the same. I have purposefully introduced the story of the school in this way: To describe my entrance as an outsider's entrance, into the school. As a white woman, raised in the Midwest with lots of land in her backyard, there are obvious characteristics that make me an outsider to FWSAG. First of all, I am white. Being white in this 99.5% black school makes me stand out. I dress differently. I talk differently. I am different. However, there are several reasons why I am not only an outsider to this place but have also become an insider.

I have been visiting to the school for two years. The teachers know who I am. The students think of me as the "science lady who likes to ask them questions". The principal hugs me and gives little gifts. I do not feel uncomfortable in the school. I know the children's names for the teachers. I know where the children are living, what they are doing, and how much these teachers worry about their children.

In the back of my mind I ask: "Shouldn't someone who is African American be researching this place?" Undoubtedly, the answer is, "Yes". However, I have been afforded the opportunity to be allowed into this school, to document what is happening. I believe because of my constant collaboration with the members of this community, there is something to be gained in this cross-cultural conversation. My hope is because I have taken every opportunity to ensure the integrity of the data and by asking good questions that the value of this study will be understood. ….

My role changes many times from feeling like an insider when a student reaches up to hold my hand to feeling like an outsider when told by a teacher, "You would not understand. That is just how *we* talk to our girls." I am challenged during both times not only to negotiate these roles but also to describe how and why what happens around me. This description of changing roles will be crucial for my data analysis in order to provide integrity for the data.

Therefore, although still in the back of my mind will constantly be, "How would this be different if the researcher were a true member of the community?" I know there is value to this type of conversation; there is value to describing the changing roles of this researcher; and there is value in including my subjectivities in my research. It is for these reasons that my role as a researcher in this situation is justified not *in spite of* but *because* of these differences, transitions, and subjectivities.

*When* Cassie *read the preceding version of her lengthy letter to me, she responded (June 24, 2011): "I love it! You cut in the perfect parts—Thanks so much." Debriefing and member checking has helped me to get this representation 'right'.*

**Veronica** pulled from four established methodologies: bricolage (Denzin & Lincoln, 2000), portraiture (Lawrence-Lightfoot, 1983), educational connoisseurship (Eisner, 1991), and appreciative inquiry (Cooperrider, Whitney, & Stavros, 2008). Each of these methodologies had contextual components found essential based on my review of research in content area literacy and preservice teachers. Therefore, I pulled these components together and formed *(Re)valuing Methodology,* in which I sought to see and understand content area literacy in a new way. What was intriguing in this process was seeing and exploring the potentials of innovative methods appropriate for the purpose of the study and the methodological aim, as well as understanding how methodology and methods impact one's form of representation. I came to see that not only do the social research processes connect and inform each other, i.e., literature review influences methodology, which influences data collection methods, which influences data representation, which in turn influences the literature, but also the use of innovative methodology, data collection methods and representation methods can lead to new ways of seeing and understanding.

LANGUAGE

**Shaunna**'s Priority Three: I learned the importance of language in QD at two of the worst points of the writing process: after the data were coded and the findings were written cohesively in "Chapter 4: Presentation of the Data", and at the final dissertation hearing. If nothing else when conducting QR, remember that language is powerful.

After spending the summer of 2009 feverishly writing Chapter 4 and submitting the complete chapter the day before my wedding to the love of my life, I returned from my honeymoon to scathing emails from my committee saying, "Dig deeper, Shaunna…the data begs for more analysis." "What does this mean?" and "Is there more to this?" As a result, I spent additional weeks reanalyzing data, recoding data, and rewriting major portions of a chapter that still had yet to see the light of day. This chaos ensued only three months prior to the targeted final dissertation hearing date.

During the final dissertation hearing, one of the first questions was a line drive from my methodologist. Given that the title of my study was "The Spiritual Development of Nonheterosexual Undergraduate Students," she wanted me to elaborate on how I chose the word "nonheterosexual" for my study and how language was a limitation for my study. To be clear, language can be a limitation for any study, yet I felt that I had conducted painstaking research concerning language that is used by LGB communities that are often oppressed by my own heterosexual community. Initially I felt betrayed, given that so many drafts had been submitted using such language, but the lesson that I took away was this: no matter what words you choose, language is loaded. Choose words and use them carefully and strategically.

When **Wanju** lost words in writing, I often listened to the interview audio clips. Listening to my participants' voices helped me to reconnect with them and helped me to go back to the time while I was interviewing them. Often I was able to continue my writing. Often I was inspired again by them. To a great extent, their words were guiding my writing and leading the direction of my research.

METHOD/OLOGY

Once **Cassandra** had my topic, I began noticing everyday occurrences, analyzing for example, why so many people get excited and have "spirited" outbursts by the end of a preached sermon at church. Believe it or not, I actually turned this phenomenon into a mini research project to get my feet wet with the QM. In trying to make sense of the whole phenomenon of "getting happy", I actually wrote out research questions: (1) What makes some folks get happy while others seem not to be affected by the preached word? and, (2) What are the effects of getting happy?

I interviewed a few of the people around me at the end of several sermons, and I also interviewed a few of my friends. (I never told anyone that these interviews were leading up to my real research and study.) I must admit, conducting this poorly constructed survey helped me understand why QR can provide rich, thick data that must be interpreted for its true meaning. Additionally, I learned the words have different meaning for different individuals. This led me to be curious about the various research designs.

Initially phenomenology struck my interest. I read as many articles as I could about the topic. I wrote research questions that fit the design. I even wrote interview questions I thought were appropriate for a phenomenological study. It was when I was preparing to defend my proposal for the second time that I discovered *asking* structured interview questions did not allow for a phenomenological approach. As a result, I had to revise my original plan and restate my methods as a single-site case study with a phenomenological approach. My methodologist and I felt it was important to allow participants to talk about what they wanted to talk about but with a few guided questions initially. I guess you could say, I dodged a bullet by using that approach.

**Jim B** used grounded theory (GT) for my study, which was in and of itself a methodological question. At least one faculty member in my department strongly recommended against using GT because it is by nature unpredictable, with the possibility that nothing of significance would emerge from the data. Thankfully others were more supportive, although I had to build a strong case for the appropriateness of GT to my research question. I did this by diving into the literature on GT as a method, as well as reading several examples of dissertations and research articles using GT. I also started reviewing the data from the national research team project I was a part of and applying the GT principles I was reading about. Doing this provided hands-on experience and also gave me preliminary findings to illustrate how the methodology fit with my data and question.

I enjoyed the organic nature of GT and was invigorated by the ways my findings evolved with each new interview via the constant comparative process. Sometimes categories that emerged became very large and broke apart into new, distinct categories. Other times, categories that seemed initially promising failed to develop and were folded into existing groups. I think this would be a very difficult and perhaps painful process for someone who desires a firmly structured course of action.

In order to bolster the trustworthiness of my findings and to help me navigate the GT process, I recruited a peer debriefer from my research team experience to review a portion of my data and provide critical feedback. I received a small grant from the Graduate School to provide compensation. The debriefer reviewed 20–25% of my data, a combination of data that I identified as difficult for me to categorize, as well as non-problematic examples selected at random. In instances where there was disagreement between us, we discussed our interpretations and resolved the discrepancy during the meeting, building upon previous examples and conversations to guide us.

## THEORETICAL FRAMEWORKS

*"Assert Yourself!" –* **Sheila** Fram's *letter (abridged and titled)*

Much of the context surrounding my experiences included a desire to obtain an interdisciplinary degree in Education. I was limited as to where I could study, financially, location-wise, etc. Partly, I chose the university because I had lived in the area and attended a high school nearby in my teens. However, no program at the university existed that shared the knowledge I knew I needed. I ended up in the Curriculum and Instruction Division in a language and literacy program, but I took courses in education, policy studies, political science, visual studies, sociology and other areas to gain that knowledge. My focus on discourses was my connection to the program. My main interest was in identifying, deconstructing, examining and understanding (as many as possible) kinds of social, cultural, language, political and epistemological ideologies.

I took many courses that included numerous social and critical theories and many kinds of data collection and analysis methods. I had much difficulty finding an advisor and committee members. After researching the backgrounds of professors in a number of colleges and departments, I met with those that had an interdisciplinary background, believing they had experiences and knowledge from which I could benefit. Some did not believe that they could help me write a dissertation; others were just overwhelmed with the students they currently had. The one that agreed to be my final advisor was a professor from whom I had taken a course, and who had the insight needed to be able to assess where I wanted to go and what I wanted to do before I thoroughly understood myself. The changing to a new advisor was frowned upon, but I did what I had to do and ignored the negative comments.

Finding the other committee members became a daunting task. Most had expertise in one or two areas, but none had multiple areas of expertise. For example, I needed someone who had a background in examining political, social, cultural and epistemological ideologies. This was not a main focus for any professor, but areas that some had examined as a part of a larger focus. I selected two professors who, I felt, had the most experience and knowledge in the field of education.

I share with you my experiences with theory and how essential it has become to be able to develop complex theoretical frameworks for QR and mixed methods research designs.

My "Review of the Literature: Socialization" section (pages 3–20) is a short and to-the-point summary of the required readings I had completed during my doctoral program before I started writing my dissertation. It does not convey to you the late-nights sitting and reading or the stressful attempts to employ a number of the theories in analyses and theoretical comparisons for course research projects. It does not convey to you the times of frustration when I just could not comprehend the scope of such new theories as Bourdieu's (1977) "habitus".

While writing my dissertation, the logical order of information that you see in this section escaped me at the time. I was so overwhelmed with theories that I lost sight of the intent of this section. My advisor was determined to get me to figure out the intent and to not just tell me the answer. The main intention of this section was to show the advancement of knowledge as an intellectual process with "growing pains" that helped me to get to the point where I could discuss why my theoretical framework was what it was. It may read as a compilation of literature on the topic of socialization, but the process of writing this section has greater meaning to me and summarizes my accomplishment of taking on all of this knowledge in order to employ social and critical perspectives when needed for an analysis stage.

One of the main difficulties I experienced while developing a theoretical framework was the conflicting perspectives of two committee members. One professor emphasized the use of grounded theory and the development of theories; the other professor emphasized the use of theories during the analysis to identify social phenomena. The introductory sentences of my theoretical framework section disguise many battles over the use of the term "sensitizing constructs". The sentences read:

My theoretical framework included the sensitizing constructs of *struggle, resistance, accommodation* and *mediation*. I used specific definitions of these concepts based on my intent to use them during the analysis of the data. (p. 27)

What resulted was an integration of the constant comparative analysis method from grounded theory and the use of a theoretical framework in order to appease both professors. I did not realize the significance of this work until later; doing both became a way to avoid being blinded by my dependence on theories. My effort to integrate has helped me do more effective analyses in mixed methods studies. Excerpts from my "Constant Comparative Analysis" section (p. 45–57) begin explaining the integration process.

Overall, learning how to develop a complex theoretical framework has helped me to become resourceful when investigating a social phenomenon. Having learned so many social and critical theories has been a major resource; I have an amazing arsenal of knowledge at my disposal when doing research. Writing the major theoretical framework section was somewhat easy because I had developed it early on with the intent to use it during the analysis process. The reasoning behind the use of specific concepts and theories and the significance of the framework was not teased out until later. I found a way to integrate grounded theory and the use of a theoretical framework, where many would avoid doing this and remain faithful to one or the other. Sincerely, Sheila.

## RELATED ISSUES

During **Katherine**'s dissertation proposal defense, two of my committee members encouraged me to further explore potential sources of biases and steps I could take to neutralize them. So, before commencing my second year of ethnographic field work, I re-visited all of my literature and created a plan of action to help me do just that. ....

To strengthen data quality, I balanced collection of official messages with those collected informally. I listened intently for outliers and followed up with participants when there was something that seemed out of place or there was something I did not understand. Additionally, I triangulated across data sources by looking for patterns across interviews, observations, and documents. Finally, I asked informants to read and comment on reported findings and have included participants' feedback in the appendices.

**Ronn** had to navigate exposure to criminal activity. For example, one of the parents frequently smoked marijuana in her bedroom while I was in the home, and one of the adolescents became involved in a gang. I also observed many positive things and wrote about how doubled-up residences had protective aspects. As a former teacher, I had to consider my responsibility in reporting these activities. After months of reflecting and seeking counsel from scholars, I decided that entering the homes was a privilege. These families gave me the opportunity to understand their lives and became vulnerable as they let down their guard. I did not report any of the incidents I observed. I did not want the families to feel judged or that I betrayed their trust.

As time progressed I also realized that I was developing close relationships with several of the adolescents and their families. I had to critically analyze my perceived boundaries between friendship and research. Actually, I continue to analyze this issue. What was my responsibility to these youth during the study and after it ended? I was given titles including friend, mentor and family. What was my responsibility to fulfill the obligation inherent in these titles? At this point I have few answers, but encourage researchers to think through their relational boundaries before entering the field and then periodically throughout the process.

The importance of participant relationships also became an integral part of **Veronica**'s dissertation process. QI demands we get close to those holding the information we desire to understand. This closeness does not happen without time and nurturing.

For **Donna**, the most difficult aspect of QR was finding the balance between objectivity and empathy. Achieving that balance between reflexivity and the need to be attentive to prior assumptions about the researched on multiple levels was a difficult concept to navigate. I constantly struggled with my biases and preconceived notions about men and masculinity; recognizing researcher power was especially important to me.

**ANON** told the participants I would do my best to keep them anonymous, yet I observed in a small school and anyone with knowledge of the school would most likely be able to identify them. I also had to sign in every day I was at the school, so the principal could have matched the days I was there with the teacher I visited and deduced which teachers I was working with. Interviews have been easier to disguise since I spoke with about half of the teachers, but I only observed in one class per grade level, so these teachers' identities are more difficult to hide. Of the four teachers I worked with, only one is still at the school, so I feel the most protective towards her. I don't feel that there would be any backlash from what they said or what I observed, but you never know how others may interpret things. These issues were discussed with the teachers up-front and most did not care if they were anonymous or not.

Since the superintendent and a few other administrators are interested in my findings, I will prepare an edited version for them that will contain less information and do a better job of maintaining anonymity than in my dissertation. One woman at the district office was concerned about remaining anonymous, but she is the only person in a certain role and her role is relevant to the study. I will remove her quotes from anything that will be seen by her superiors.

Something **ANON** struggled with after the fact was anonymity and providing the district with feedback. As I wrote and analyzed the data, it became very difficult to explain strengths and weaknesses (for lack of better terms at this point) while maintaining confidentiality. For example, analysis made it immediately obvious who was responsible. Further analysis discussed the other participants' roles.

How could I communicate these findings effectively back to the district without "selling out" some and pointing to others?

I am ashamed to say I ended up not giving the district anything in the end – which fortunately coincided with the retirement and turnover of several participants, leaving my work the least of their concerns. I would never advocate what I did, but to others in this process, be more aware than I of these issues at the start of the study and consciously plan for what information you will be willing to share back with the participants.

The final stages of the study raised an ethical issue. **Ronn** wanted to conduct member checks with the participants, but my analysis of the data suggested that two of the youth would likely not succeed in high school or transition to postsecondary education. Offering the participants an opportunity to read my work would allow for an informative discussion about my perceptions of their lives. However, what might be the consequences of telling a teenager you do not think he or she will graduate high school? I decided to give each participant vignettes I had written focused on how they spent time and their experiences in the educational system. However, I did not provide them with copies of my analysis. The risk of potential harm was too great.

**Amy** didn't anticipate how my personal relationships with the teachers I worked with might color my interpretation and analysis. In classes, we were always cautioned about this and I thought I understood, but after spending a few months in a site and seeing teachers weekly, it was difficult to separate and view them as "subjects". I find that when I am writing things up now, I feel a bit guilty when I include something that might be viewed as negative by some.

**Sandy**'s committee wanted me to be explicit in my writing regarding issues of validity and reliability, which I addressed by establishing and following a detailed interview protocol.

One member of **Mary**'s committee suggested I construct relational tables/charts to increase method validity for the committee skeptic. Mine related questions, concepts and methods! I believe they do assist with focus and clarity. **Carita**'s committee encouraged the use of tables and graphs to provide a visual picture for the reader. The NVivo software progam helped to formulate tables and graphs from the narratives I downloaded into the program from Word. I formatted the tables and graphs according to the APA guidelines once the data were analyzed.

**Corey**'s question was "how much data is too much?" "How do I know when to quit?" I had dozens of interviews, observations, surveys, videos, curriculum, and more. It was overwhelming. I would constantly ask my advisors, "When do I stop collecting?" Their response did not help either, "You will know." "What? What do you mean 'I will know?'" What kind of answer was that?

Well, you know what? They were right. There came a point in my collection that I knew I had enough, and I was done. Plus, I was also done driving to my research site, which was in a different town from where I lived and where my university was located.

> **Nancy**'s *original email, below, mentioned "the self-reflection piece". I wrote back, requesting further information. I place her explanations here, to foreshadow our proximity to Section Five, about writing.*

**"Self as instrument"**. I wrote the self-reflection piece. I felt it was necessary, and it helped eliminate any concern for bias my committee may have had. I enjoyed writing it very much. As I wrote, my study evolved into something I became very proud of and was eager to defend. I think had I not done this piece, I would have had some self-doubt.

*Nancy: Was this piece required of you? Did someone suggest it? Is it in the thesis?*

Those of us who were completing a qual study were asked to complete it as part of our research. The intent was to help us find any hidden bias that may be a manifestation of our personal experiences.

The piece was titled "Self as Instrument". It was included in the research methods section of my dissertation. The piece helped me to identify things about myself that I may inadvertently project onto the study findings. Opening myself up in the piece also let my committee know that I had explored my personal feelings about the topic and had used caution when making assumptions about the findings.

I think the study could have gone very differently had I not done it. I had a difficult time getting my topic through my committee, since they felt it was controversial. The reflection piece helped them to see that I was sincere about wanting to open the topic up to discovery and discussion and that I did not have any preconceived ideas about what it was that I intended to write. I think I would have had more push back had I not done the piece.

I wrote the section fairly early on in my study, and it really helped me gain clarity. I learned things about myself that I think every researcher should want to know. This self-discovery helped me to think more deeply about my topic. I immersed myself to a degree that I hadn't imagined previously, which helped me gain greater insight into the experiences of my participants and the importance of the topic.

At the end of **Kj**'s dissertation I wrote about the QR process, that I had a new appreciation for the work and rigor associated with it. When I present and share the data analysis steps I followed, there seems to be a better appreciation within my doctoral cohort for the qual process.

## CONCLUSION

**Shaunna**'s Priority Four: Doing "whatever makes sense" for your dissertation. As a linear thinker, it was futile to think that my laundry lists of questions for my committee during the writing process would be answered as succinctly as they were asked. Instead, the consistent refrain I heard from my dissertation committee chairperson was "Whatever makes sense!" I initially interpreted this response as being dismissed by him. Instead, that refrain became liberating. Such freedom allowed me to craft a 'do-it-yourself' dissertation. It provided me the freedom to make thoughtful choices about everything related to my dissertation, but also required me to use very clear and specific language to defend such decisions.

As mentioned previously, the "Chapter 4: Presentation of Data" was initially a major struggle. To meet my institution's requirements, I was expected to briefly describe how the data were analyzed, organize the raw data into logical themes, and define the themes. As my document mentioned, "Although the information in this chapter is presented in an organized fashion for the reader, the data did not neatly respond to each research question as originally posited" (Payne Gold, 2010, p. 113). Overall, my decisions considered what made sense to me and what would make sense to an outside reader who would be familiar with my study.

# WRITING ABOUT WRITING

The most important thing **Sandy** learned was to actually START writing.

## INTRODUCTION

Although the correspondents reflected about the writing-thinking-doing-learning process at many points in their letters, this section of the book focuses on the contributions that specifically deal with writing, at some length.

A big part of **Kristen**'s experience is what I can only call "readiness." It was strange; I had kicked around (and around, and around, and around…) the same dissertation idea over and over again, from different angles, and with different people for months (it was a couple of years, actually). I was interested in the topic, I had used the ideas in a couple of small-scale studies, I had read some of the literature, and I even wanted to finish my program. But I wasn't "ready." I would sit down to think about it, to write, to draft an outline…and nothing. I think a big part of writing your dissertation is being ready to write it, although I have no data and no other experiences to back up this belief. I am not really sure how to explain it. For a long time, I was dissertation-avoidant. Then, one day, things just seemed to "click" and now all I want to do is work on my dissertation—to write it, to read for it, to think about it, to talk about it (of course, now, I find that I have massive piles of other work to kick through, just to get to my dissertation…). Before I was "ready", there were certain books that had sat on my shelves for months and months and I just could not pick them up (or, if I did manage to get one off of the shelf, I'd read about five sentences, decide it wasn't a good use of my time, and move on to something else). Now, I can't put these same books down. They make so much sense. I find so much value in each of them. It's strange, though; at the same time, I can't imagine having pushed them away for so long, but I also know that they would not have had the same meaning or made the same sense to me, had I read them way back when I first bought them. This is not to say, of course, that one should not work hard throughout the whole process. I did work hard. I thought and talked about my topic and my approach, generally, far more than I was comfortable with. I talked about it so much in school settings that I could not talk about it in my home life; even now, my close friends and family know only a skeleton outline of "what my dissertation is about." So my transition from "not ready" to "ready" did not come about in the absence of hard work. Nor does it mean that there is not a lot of hard work still to come.

There is, however, at least for me, a different mindset from which I seem to approach that hard work, now that I feel I am "ready" for my dissertation.

**Corey:** The frustration and need to be finished came in several stages. First came the lack of motivation to write. It was difficult to sit and write for hours and hours every single day. There was a time of 'dissertation writer's block.' I went nearly 2 months without writing a single thing or even looking at it. I was done. Then I realized that I was close and needed to be done. Finally, I told my committee that I wanted to defend by the end of the fall semester. It took some coercing, but they agreed and I worked my butt off for 4 solid months to be ready.

As **Sandy** collected data from my different sites I started identifying the themes I wanted to write about. I developed an outline for the first case study and wrote it up. My committee liked it so I was able to use the same format for the other two case studies. I found this very helpful as far as organizing the data and writing it up in an organized way. With transcription data from multiple sources, it could have been overwhelming. I used ATLAS.ti to assemble coded data. Even though many passages overlapped, it was a useful way to organize the data so I could interpret and analyze it.

    **Vic** began my adventure during the QR course of my doctoral program. At the close of the course I wrote an abbreviated research proposal and was almost certain I had developed some thoughts and content that would end up in my dissertation. Didn't use a thing! The foundation had been laid, but the eventual writing was far removed from that original document. (As a student who was also a full time practitioner, I was concerned about conservation of effort, which was probably a naïve way to approach writing.)

The final draft of **Nancy**'s study looks nothing like the first draft – things changed so much after each set of interview questions that I continued to both refine and to broaden my study. I learned I cannot get attached to anything I have written because the next day an entire chapter may have to be tossed and replaced with something more meaningful. Rely on people who trust the method and use them to be another set of eyes! Numbers are numbers, but words have multiple layers of meaning.

**Ginny** had always been told I was a talented writer, but that impression was immediately put to the test when developing Chapter One. I felt I knew what I wanted to study, had a fairly large amount of knowledge about the related areas, and therefore, putting all of that into Chapter One should not be too difficult. After all, I had written dozens and dozens of papers before and taught composition, so I imagined myself having an upper hand with the whole writing part of the dissertation. Boy, was that illusion shattered when I received back from my advisor the first draft of my Chapter One! I had never seen so many edits, comments, and deletions on any of my papers before, e.g., "What did you mean by this? Expand on this. Citation needed here. This does not belong here, maybe you can use it elsewhere? More skepticism needed. Do not use "this" or "that" or "there exists". Do not use clichés/ colloquialisms. Write the story of the literature, not reality. Question what you read; do not buy into the propaganda!"

The more I wrote, the more I had to change. At first, I tried to embrace the edits and felt challenged by the comments to write better. However, I was not prepared for, nor was I used to, someone challenging my writing so deeply and thoroughly before. After about the fourth or fifth re-write, I became quite discouraged. I had made so many changes that I questioned whether this was actually my study any more. To top it off, as I read more and more on my topic and wrote more, I could feel the direction changing. New ideas developed in my mind and new questions were forming in response. It was an uncomfortable feeling. I was beginning to feel like I had wasted a lot of time writing a bunch of material that was not going to be included in the final cut. Until this time, most of the communication with my advisor had been through emails, but now I felt I needed to schedule a face-to-face meeting.

We met over lunch. I described some of the new things I was reading in academic journals and finally told him that I was confused by all of the information and unsure as to how to put it all together now. He asked me if I could feel my work changing; I nodded my head scared and excited at the same time. I was a black and white kind of person. Tell me what to do and I will do it, but this was different. The more I "did" reading and writing, the more it changed into something that required more reading and more writing. I felt like there was no end to it, and, therefore, no sense of accomplishment at reaching the goal of completion. It was just like Socrates said, "The more you learn, the more you realize how little you know." I admitted my frustration to my advisor who assured me that this was part of the process and natural to experience. I am a progress type of person, so when I do not see forward motion, I am uneasy.

This learning to be patient with my developing ideas, writing and weaving together the story I wanted to learn, and how I wanted to study it, was the most difficult part of my journey.

I encountered similar frustrations as I wrote Chapter Two, looking to support my ideas with the research of others in a cohesive "story of the lit" without my comments or bias on how I thought things were or should be.


**Keith** found chapters 1-3 particularly grueling to write. I found no enjoyment in writing a LR. But the moment I conducted my first interview, things began to change. After that, I seemed to muster a resurgence of energy and determination. Looking back, I think it had little to do with completing my project. It had more to do with getting my participants' voice out.

*Don't let this paragraph fool you; Keith has, literally, a longer story to tell.*

When I look at my transcript, I stand in horror as to just how far back I started my degree. Let's just say, I was pushing the 10 year time limit set by my institution. That being said, I finished my coursework in what I perceive as a timely manner.

But I floundered on my dissertation. Once I completed my coursework, it was nearly 4 years to the day when I defended. And my topic wasn't some stale area that my committee appointed to me. I loved my topic. I had ownership over it. However, the roadblocks seemed to be this odd combination of approach-avoidant behavior and obsessive-compulsive disorder. . . . .

On the approach-avoidant end—I had to fight myself to work at writing. Most suggest setting realistic goals and blocks of time to write every day. But my contention is this: you can set all the realistic goals you want, but if you are not *honest* with yourself, you will never achieve those goals. By honesty, I mean setting aside everything you read about writing a dissertation and being critically honest at how you—yourself—operates, conceptualizes things, and how long it takes you to write.

On the obsessive-compulsive end…well…if my obsessive-compulsive tendencies were directed towards the dissertation writing, I would have been finished an eternity ago! Unfortunately, my obsessive-compulsive tendencies gravitate towards things like Xbox 360, Playstation 3, etc. It got to the point where a friend of mine removed all my beloved gaming consoles from my house, and my sister changed my passwords to my video game account, just so I could finish writing.

**Kristan** rewrote chapter four – my data presentation chapter FOUR TIMES. It was totally painful at the time, but the experience of meaningfully rewriting this chapter encouraged me to play with my data and take real ownership over it. I know that at times I was a little tentative about really "owning" my work because I was, of course, trying to make sure that it met my advisor's requirements. Rewriting those chapters, even though it was tough to reconceptualize, was worth it. I think that experience, in particular, helped me to learn to be a better advisor to the students that I work with now.

Writing became the bridge that connected the analysis and findings construction in **Angela LV**'s dissertation. Through writing, I tackled both the analysis of the data and the connections between data pieces. By "writing" I do not mean an academic account of the study – at least not during the first attempts – but rather the engagement in examining my thoughts via producing text, even when that first text was in the form of a very personal, and inarticulate, but honest interpretation of the pieces of data so far. Writing helped me tap into levels of analysis that I could not reach by just thinking, writing codes on the margins of an observation or interview, making tables, or taking notes out of context. The *act of writing* became the link between the analysis of my data and the construction of the findings. Through writing, I reached the understanding that the findings did not emerge from the data through refined codes, but rather from putting the story together. And as a researcher, I had all the power – and the responsibility – to support that story with the data I reported. When I came across this understanding, I embraced the idea that during analysis I could not help but write, because writing was the channel of my thinking and of my analysis. When writing/analyzing, I was able to more consciously examine the analytical choices I was making, and thus look for ways to make it more systematic, by forcing myself to move through similar layers of analysis with each participant and with each source of information. . . . .

Through the solitary and painstaking time of dissertation writing, **Angela LV** gained a great deal of understanding of what it takes to produce a QR report. I learned that producing each piece of the dissertation – contrary to what most Ph.D. students often fantasize about – did not always depend on a deadline. Many times I said to myself "I HAVE to get this chapter done by Friday, or else!" Most times, the self-inflicted pressure of the deadline had the opposite effect on me! Instead of pushing me to write, it caused me to hide from writing and to accumulate overwhelming feelings of anxiety. Less important tasks, like answering e-mails from friends, organizing my home library, and even painting a couple of walls often took priority! A day before the deadline, and without much progress done in between, I either felt it was too late to work on it and did not write, or glued myself to the computer for a whole day, struggling with writing and guilt, and a sheer desire to be doing something else! By the Friday deadline, I had neither finished the section I set out to finish, nor was I feeling satisfied. The compounding feeling of anxiety made me realize that the "deadline approach" was not appropriate for me.

I experimented with setting up a routine of daily writing (Bolker, 1998). I started by writing 45 minutes every day, making my writing a mandatory way to start my day. Being a morning person helped me. The timed-writing approach made me forget about deadlines for a while. It was surprising to me how much writing I could produce in a 45-minute focused writing period! At the end of the 45 minutes, I had jotted down some written ideas that, although still raw and unedited, I could continue working on during other timed periods during the day. The kitchen timer became (and still is) my best friend when it came to writing! I find that focused timed writing alleviates the feeling of having to be glued to the chair the whole day to produce some text. Once the timed writing routine was established, it was easy to increase the writing time to two or three hours a day, and to see the progress in my writing. It was the compound effect that made a difference between not finishing and finishing the QD.

**Angela LV**'s *writing throughout this text should give heart to her ESL colleagues. She continues:*

Writing is hard for most graduate students, but I can confidently say that writing academically in English is particularly hard for people whose native language is not English. I am one in that group. My native language provides a solid conceptual base that allows me to understand the structure of academic text, but I have to grapple with how to most effectively communicate my thoughts in ways that read academically, yet, appealing and creatively in my second language. Not an easy job. As a result, added to my regular work of writing to think and rethink the data to produce a decent finding, was the work of reading and rereading the work of others in the search for models of writing that could feed my own. Extensive reading for academic writing models, as much as reading for information, is a necessary component of the dissertation work for ESL Ph.D. students.

Another thing **Wanju** found extremely beneficial toward becoming a good writer was reading novels such as *Little Women* (Alcott, 1868; 1872) and *The Portrait of Dorian Grey* (Wilde, 1961). This might be just a tip for non-native English speakers. There are also vocabularies that a person has to learn to be a good qual researcher. I learn them by reading other people's dissertations, journal articles, etc. Mostly, I learn by doing. The more I write the better/more comfortable I become with words.

## CONCLUSION

**Cindy** *writes:* The most important moral of our collective stories is tenacity and positive self-talk. Tell yourself every day, "I can do this! If I work on it, at least an hour every day, it will eventually be done." The *Little Engine That Could* (1961; 1990) is a good reminder for the QD journey. Often I would say out loud, "I think I can. I think I can. I think I can." Then I would sit down for my hour and often get so involved it would be two or three hours later when I stopped.

# "IN THE END…"

**Rich** was thrown a curve ball during graduate school and that was falling in love with a quantitative researcher. By quant I don't mean simply some surveys and secondary data analysis, I mean programming code in sophisticated stats programs because SPSS isn't "good enough," and generating ever-higher levels of abstraction. I firmly believe that the debates the two of us have had over the years – about the applicability of particular methodologies and the pros and cons of various methods of inquiry – have been more beneficial to me than any amount of research I have done in the QR literature. That isn't to devalue the latter, but rather to espouse the incredible value of the former. Call it a "thought partner" or an intellectual sparring partner, our conversations have resulted in rock solid methodologies and justifications for undertaking a qual approach.

This approach has also helped me to be able to write qual papers in the language of quant research – using tables and doing some aggregation of data for example – that both assuaged my committee and pushed me to think about the boundaries of QR. By this I don't mean "how can we make qual work look more quant," but rather, "how can we make that case that both are complementary and essential?"

## INTRODUCTION

Section Six is the final portion of this book. With it I attempt to bring closure to topics that are ongoing and vary in importance as you experience and learn through them. As more than several correspondents attest, there *is* an ending, there is "life after" the qualitative thesis or dissertation. We hope you have found encouragement for your progress and reinforcement for the belief that you, too, can complete this work both thoughtfully and well.

### QUESTION SEVEN: IS THERE ANYTHING ELSE YOU WOULD LIKE TO TELL?

**Angela F** might tell about the day of my proposal hearing when the maintenance folks at my apartment complex painted my door shut and I had to call emergency workers to get me out in time for my hearing – but I am not sure there would be a wonderful lesson in there other than to just really try to be clear about what you can control and what you can't and the importance of greeting the work with passion and positive energy.

## THE DEFENSE

**Aaron**'s dissertation committee chair is very traditional. When I sent him the first draft of my slides for the defense presentation along with my presenter's notes, he was very concerned. He thought there was way too much text and didn't want me reading my notes. While I had no intention of reading my notes, he made it very clear that my slides should have just a couple of words to get me started and then, with NO NOTES, I should provide all the details. He said he had attended a few defenses as a committee member where students used some notes or 3 × 5 cards, but he said, "Not my students" so I really had to prepare for the defense. He reminded me that the committee had read the dissertation already; they wanted to hear me talk about it. He also told me this was not going to be a "gotcha" affair, that it should be a conversation about the research between near colleagues. Once I realized this experience was just a platform for people to have to listen to my research for an hour or so, the whole event was de-mystified. I was able to prepare with what I would want to know about the research: the problem and purpose, the methodology and research process, and my findings.

I took Monday off after the defense, had lunch with some colleagues, nice Mexican food, and a dinner with my family, some good ribs! Now it is just back to the grind and figuring out which project and paper I want to tackle first.

**Megan** found it to be a humbling experience that so many students agreed to participate in dissertation research, agreeing to make themselves vulnerable all over again; it was just as humbling to hear the students speak about what they had learned from their experience. And finally, on March 19, 2009 – my birthday and a year and two days after my proposal defense – I defended my dissertation to a crowd of 20+ people: friends, family, and strangers. I passed with no further revisions. Many of the recommendations brought forth by the students have been, or are in the process of being, implemented. I know that the details, depth, and true reflections would not have been realized in a study utilizing another research method.

## SINCE THE DEFENSE

Since my dissertation, **Kristan** has done things like analyzing rap videos and other pop culture artifacts. I never would have been able to do that using quant research.

When **Tiffany** does a formal presentation on my dissertation, people do not hold back with questions! I have been asked about how I dealt with subjectivity and having emotional ties and background with the topic. I have also been asked to back up my claim that I "transcended local contexts". I have also been asked to explain my method of analysis in greater detail.

**Mary** is able to apply concepts and ideas in my daily job as part of the Provost's Office of Institutional Assessment. I have developed some confidence in my approaches to work and am better at explaining them to others.

**Carin** has used the interview techniques of rapport building specifically when I meet with students or have conversations with parents in person or on the phone. I find myself using a similar style, i.e., using open-ended questions, listening attentively, and utilizing probing questions to gather more information. Going into the research team project, I had no idea of the impact the training would have on my future dissertation research as well as my practice as a student affairs administrator.

**Keith** is finding a common theme with all things dissertation related – I either do not know how to begin, or I become completely lost within my own writing once I get going. Although I speak of my dissertation in the present tense, the crafting of that monstrous undertaking is complete. I successfully defended and graduated in the fall 2010 semester. However, I am finding that the dissertation – the topic, the literature, and, indeed, anything associated with I it – is far from over after you have defended and graduated.

Lately, it seems that my dissertation is revisiting my life as if it were some ghostly apparition visiting my bedside at night. I thought I was home free after I participated in commencement (which I attended kicking and screaming. After sitting in class and writing for 7 years, I could not stomach the thought of sitting for even an hour more. But my parents laid down the guilt trip on this one, so I went.). But not long into the start of the spring semester, my former dissertation adviser contacted me. "Are you ready for the next step?" she asks, "are you ready to start thinking about what pieces to pull for some presentations and articles?"

Despite my understanding of how the dissertation eventually might lead one to publish a cache of articles, I somehow had mentally, emotionally, and conceptually shut that door. I have probably been thinking once that last word was scribbled down and that last thought was conceptualized, I was done. More importantly, I did not want to revisit it. Yet, my dissertation continues to haunt me. I am revisiting, re-tweaking, and re-tooling portions of it and submitting those sections as proposals to conferences, all of which seems to be the norm, but I somehow find it grueling to do so.

The thing **Liz** most struggled with, and still does, is moving from a QD into qual manuscripts for publication. I was a quant researcher before this endeavor and have a pretty good grasp on turning quantitative analysis into manuscript form. However, "results" in QR are a different beast – how do you present data? Findings? Analysis? This is very challenging. I had two manuscripts I really wanted to result from my work – one finally went out (2 years later) in the fall and one is eating away at my desk and has been since I graduated.

Everything I have written is about double the appropriate length. I struggle with cutting it down while preserving richness and validity. My greatest revelation is that you need to establish the rigor of your methodology (reliability, validity, analytical methods) and then move straight into major findings – with little presentation of analysis in between, whereas in a quant manuscript you present the results of the analysis – a table for example – and summarize it before moving into discussion. I recommend using other scholars with experience writing QR to review your work, but be prepared because EVERYONE does it differently and the feedback you get is likely to differ significantly.

On the positive side, I wrote and defended my dissertation and used it to secure an academic position at a research university. My previous record using statistics makes me an attractive research partner but so does my dissertation, which represented to most that I have capacity to design and conduct QR. My decision to put question before method has led to some interesting research projects and relationships that otherwise would not have been possible.

At **Michele**'s current position, I feel neither a sense of support nor a lack of support for QR. I am teaching at a small, private university and the focus seems to be more on teaching than research. I recently presented at a state research poster session, however, and was the only qual researcher there. That felt a bit strange, considering the university I attended was very heavily oriented toward QR.

Two months after **Ronn** finalized the dissertation, I found myself in a faculty position as a dissertation chair. I had not expected such a quick transition, and I was surprised by how much I had actually learned about the process. Here are a few bits of advice:

- The most important thing to remember is that conducting a QS is a privilege. The researcher gets the rare opportunity to enter another person's life. The entire process should be viewed not as laborious, but as an amazing honor.
- The research question drives the entire study – the methodology should respond to the question(s).
- After my first meeting with a graduate student I ask him/her to think through the following questions and have a justification before our next meeting:
  - Why are you choosing this methodology? What are its basic tenets? Its strengths and weaknesses? Has it been used previously with this or a similar population? What did they find? What challenges did they have? Is your study breaking any new ground?
  - What data are going to be collected? In what time frame? Are you doing a trial run of the instruments or does this build on previous work? How will your data be analyzed? How will your reader know the data are valid or trustworthy? …Do you hold any biases or assumptions?
  - How will your data be stored? How will you avoid coercion? How will you protect the participants?

**Shaunna:** Final thoughts. My dissertation catapulted my endeavors as a scholar-practitioner into various areas of teaching, research, and service. The study helped me to parlay meager teaching experience into a professorial lecturer position. I have continued to pursue LGB research while publishing literature concerning the various perspectives of spirituality and sexuality. Finally, I have been honored to serve on my institution's President's Commission for LGBT Issues. My work has even won a campus award. However, none of these results could replace the amount of righteous indignation that I have developed when witnessing injustice, especially concerning members of LGB and T communities. I have risked my ordination as a minister in my denomination to 'call out' clergy colleagues who were ignorant and complicit in the oppression of those who are not heterosexual. Combating such micro- and macro-aggressions provides additional peace of mind. I now know that I have conducted the best study possible, on the most expeditious timeline that was genuine, authentic, and life-altering. If nothing else, this type of academic integrity always 'makes sense'.

*Once again, I choose to put a 'whole person' in front of you, below, because the context of your work is beyond your desk, office, home. As I told you in the description of my analysis (see Appendix I), it seems I was either unable or somehow kept myself from "getting"* **Michele***'s experiences when I first read her letter. It was only later, when I was finally able to let the letters stand for themselves and honor each individual one at a time, that I allowed myself to feel what she was telling me; hence the title of our almost final words, below.*

APPRECIATING OUR "TEXT" – OUR LIVES, OUR SELVES, OUR EXPERIENCING

*"Behind the Words"* – **Michele** Paynter Paise (*unabridged, my title)*

A final area of difficulty was the time it took to complete my dissertation. This was more of a personal issue, but worth mentioning for other doctoral students who may experience something similar. During my last year on campus, I chose to be a teaching assistant for the choral department and the music education department. This meant that I was teaching two courses while taking my own coursework, collecting data from the participants in my study, and applying for jobs. My plan was to finish the dissertation before moving away and beginning my first university position. I was not able to accomplish this.

For my first job, I was hired ABD and was asked to direct a choir in addition to my responsibilities as a music education professor. I was also told that I must finish my dissertation by the end of my second year at that institution. Moving to a new place and starting a new job are stressful. I worked on my dissertation, but did not make very good progress that first year. I was also assigned a new advisor. To make matters worse, my husband did not like the area where we had moved and decided to accept a job nearly 3,000 miles away. I began the second year at this position with the determination that I would finish the document and look for a new position where I could be near my husband.

Things were going well. I was finishing my literature review and had done a great deal of writing. I applied for several positions that were closer to my husband and was looking forward to having the dissertation "out of my hair" so that I could get on with my career. My husband and I had a nice visit over Christmas break, but shortly after that, I received a call from my mother telling me that my father was very ill. I flew back to my hometown to see him and he died a few days later. Two weeks after that, I was rushed to the emergency room with pancreatitis. It was a particularly bad case. I received two blood transfusions and almost died. I was in and out of the hospital for the next four months and was told that I would need to take at least a year off of work in order to fully recover. During those four months, I was unable to eat and lost all my hair. I had trouble walking and doing other things that people often take for granted.

I had no choice but to leave my position and move to the city where my husband was living. Thankfully, I was able to teach part time and work on my dissertation during my year of recovery. As I began to feel stronger, I applied for a position in this new city. I was hired for that position and completed my dissertation during my first semester there. Sadly, my mother passed away three weeks before my graduation.

I tell this story because there were two people who kept me focused on my dissertation when I wanted to quit (and there were many times I wanted to quit): My husband and my advisor. Since I now lived very far away from campus, I had a phone appointment with my advisor every Thursday at 1:00. Sometimes we talked for 10 minutes and sometimes we talked for an hour, but we always talked. This made me stay focused. I always looked forward to being able to tell her what I accomplished; I recommend this for others who decide to move away before their dissertation is complete.

At my doctoral defense, one of the members of my committee raised an interesting question regarding some of my data collection. For example, I obtained some information about my participants from Facebook, Myspace, and other social network sites. The question concerned the ethics of using this information. I answered that I thought this method of data collection was ethical if I obtained it from what was posted on the participants' public profile. Now I am not so sure. This may be an area we need to address as qualitative researchers. I am thankful that Facebook did not exist when I was a beginning teacher. I might not want others to know certain information I might have foolishly posted at age 22. I now suspect that some of the participants may also feel the same way in a few years.

After four and a half years of data collection and writing, through many of life's challenges, my dissertation ended up being fairly traditional. At the beginning, I had big dreams that it would be highly artistic. For example, one of the participants in my study, "Chad," enjoyed performing more than teaching. I wanted to tell his story in the form of a Broadway playbill. It took so much time to sift through data and determine what was important, that I eventually just wanted the document to be done. I did make it somewhat "artsy" by weaving quotes from Lewis Carroll's *Alice in Wonderland* into various chapters, but by the end, I really just wanted to finish … artistic or not.

I wish there were some magic formula about writing a QD that I could share with others. It is a process that has to be experienced to be fully understood.

I will close this letter with a few last thoughts about my dissertation. Once I scheduled my defense, I knew that I was almost finished. I was relieved when my committee welcomed me back to the room, adding the title "Doctor" to my name. My joy lasted only a few seconds when I learned of the revisions. My defense was exactly two months before graduation, and I worked on my revisions nearly every day of those two months. My mother died during that time and her funeral was 800 miles from where I was living. I took a few days off from writing and then resumed working on revisions in the hotel room while traveling back home from her funeral. When I graduated, I put a framed photograph of my parents in my purse so that they could be with me on my big day. Graduating was both celebratory and melancholy. When my bound dissertation arrived in the mail, I put it on the shelf. The first time I opened it was to look through it to write you this letter. Thank you so much for doing this. Michele

FINAL WORDS?

Now that **Monica** is close to the end, I feel like I have completion within my grasp. I have told everybody that I don't feel that I needed to be smart, just persistent. I just need to keep on task and work towards the goal of dissertation completion. Thinking about the whole dissertation was overwhelming, but breaking up and setting short goals for myself helped immensely.

In hindsight, **Vic** now realizes that the type of written report should be dependent upon the data and analysis rather than any preconceived notions. We students tend to want structure and direction.

**Amanda** learned that QR is an iterative process – through saturation and beyond if needed. *Amen, Amanda!*

**Jim O** *writes that* my desire would be for you, the readers, to understand the strength and power that QR provides as a tool. Using QM enabled me to draw upon my own life as a source of support/strength. Additionally, a qual approach enabled me to recognize/ appreciate certain things the participants told me, because I had similar experiences.

The doctoral process was extremely stressful in that there seemed to be so much that was out of my control. **Angela F** must say that times got really challenging mostly because, I realize now, I was pushing myself to prove myself worthy. I had not yet found a balance with my own inalienable value and the work I was doing. It was not until I was through the turmoil of the doctoral process that I could grasp the words of the professor who first encouraged me to seek a Ph.D.: distinguish what you do for yourself, what you do for your career, and what you do for the cause. His advice helps me sometimes to see clearly where tensions might be occurring in my life.

**Kj** can remember constantly reflecting over my research and waking up at 3:00 AM in the morning recoding something or going back over my coding because I had forgotten some theme that came to me in the middle of the night. In the end, when I present…the data analysis steps I took (p. 91–2), there seems to be better appreciation within my cohort for the qualitative process.

## DON'T GIVE UP ON DATA!

The story of **Rich**'s dissertation is really about not wasting data. Much of the qual data in my dissertation was collected over a three year period, though the "official" dissertation work only lasted about 12 months. I originally worked on the service station paper in 2006–2007 (I defended in 2010), and set the data aside. That project started as an assignment. When it was time to write my dissertation, I realized how I needed to frame the data to make a valuable contribution to the field. I ended up nesting the information within the field of business decision making.

Of course, it wasn't just that easy! I had to collect more data, but when I re-entered the field to collect data from additional participants, much of the groundwork was already done, making it easier to complete the project. I found that a few years away from my notes and transcripts gave me a fresh perspective, ultimately resulting in a much better paper, and perhaps the basis for my future research agenda.

## SHOW YOUR DECISION MAKING ABILITY!

Having been through the defense process, **Rich** feels that my committee wanted to see that I could make good research decisions when moving from the proposal to the written/final document. This doesn't mean that I was casual about adhering to what I proposed, but it is research, and things happen. I ultimately had to change a few things about my work, including the sample size, and which sources of data I used. When I had to adjust, I didn't go back to my committee to ask their permission, rather I moved forward and included my justification for doing so in the text of my dissertation. I honestly believe that this resulted in my committee respecting my work more in the end, and they felt better about "sending me out into the world" as a researcher with a research degree.

## CONCLUSION

Enjoy the journey! **Jessie** has come to appreciate that QI challenges us to look, listen, and feel the world around us. I am amazed by the many aspects of life I did not consider prior to becoming deeply engaged in this type of work.

**Monica Jean** *writes:* In the end, it was apparent to me that QI was necessary to get at the heart of matter I was examining; numbers only would have told me so much. The conversations I had with my participants were not only relevant to answering my research questions, but also powerful tales that could not have possibly reached the readers in any other way.

On **Corey**'s final day of travel to UCSB, I had 4 copies of my dissertation. One copy stayed with the Graduate office; the other 3 went to the library to be bound. My walk back to the car empty handed was the single best feeling in the world. I walked, or should I say floated, with a gigantic weight lifted from my shoulders. I was done. The 2½-hour drive home was surreal, satisfying, wonderful, with a true sense of accomplishment.

*To Corey, and everyone here within and "there" as reader – I could not have said it better myself. Phew!*

# APPENDIX I

The story of my analysis and the more than several iterations of this book continues from page 1 in the introduction. To review, I had all letters punched and ready to read on April 1, 2011 (no joke!). My description of that thinking-working-doing-rethinking-redoing-letting go and grabbing on is here for your consideration.

ANALYSES

I have been reading my correspondents ever since that day. More importantly, I have been listening to them; that is one reason I wanted Wanju's reflection to lead our book. The correspondents helped me learn that this is not your 20th century qualitative inquiry anymore. Just two weeks ago, the last week in May, 2011, I borrowed my college's 3rd edition *Handbook of Qualitative Research* (Denzin & Lincoln, 2005) and reread the preface, introduction, and chapter one. I wanted to see if what I was thinking and feeling about what was happening "out there" through the letters was evidenced in the forward thinking volume. To my great joy, complexity lives! The correspondents describe some of the words, ideas, connections, and disjunctures discussed in those pages. Further, their level of investment in QR as a life-changing, contribution-enabling process is so powerful that my first thought back at the end of that first day was to simply submit the letters, all 69 of them, to be published "as is", an idea I now call "draft one". I could not see anything to do; I did not want to touch them. They were perfect, more than I could have asked for, both literally and figuratively.

While rereading the letters a second time the following day, starting with the last letter and reading forward, I realized that some aspects of our experiencing have remained the same over time. I knew I would have to do the work of sorting out the shared and common from that which is also experienced but perhaps not as often expressed, or expressed in this way, or that. The words of my correspondents – yes, I have to call them "my" – became a part of my thinking, looking, and choosing. The second draft of the book, therefore, became exactly that, i.e., my selections of their ideas with my wrap-around thoughts, connectors, interjections and musings. On Friday, May 13, 2011, (I sure knew how to pick my days, didn't I?:) I sent every correspondent my "version" of what I thought I would keep from their writing within a context of my sensemaking. In some places I combined correspondents' thoughts, or compared and contrasted them, as if doing so were *their* point. Feeling proud to have met my self-imposed due date, I attended graduation the next day. I spent the day after that, Sunday, prepping for the two week, intense introduction to educational research class I was to begin teaching Monday morning, which meant no book work for two weeks.

I took the Saturday after the class ended to switch gears, returning on Memorial Day Sunday to the complete draft document. I began by reading the pile of unremarked upon originals again, starting in the middle and reading to the end, then forward from the middle to the beginning. (By now I had read each letter, whole and unmarked upon, at least 7 times, not counting the times I was working with an individual's thinking, alone.) I was stunned with what two weeks away had done to me. I found myself laughing with Corey or Sarah, smiling at Cindy. Then I got to Michele's letter, which I know I had both read and certainly cognitively processed at least four times before. And there I was on the living room couch, with her letter on top of the pile of 68 others in that huge notebook, crying my eyes out, my heart and mind having finally been reached together. I was touched completely, one person to another. What was happening to me? And what did that mean for the book I had "finished"?

The answer was obvious. I was finally, for the *first* time, meeting my correspondents on their terms, not mine – not for what I hoped to find before I ever read a letter, not for what I saw/did not see/was unwilling to acknowledge in those first read-throughs, and certainly not for what I ignored/dismissed when I *did* see it. Whether we want to or not, we bring ourselves and our needs/desires/ hopes and expectations into the 'reading' of our context/the data, whatever that is/ they are. This is not a new idea, but it is amazingly simple not to 'get it' the first go arounds. I suspect that is what our first bouts of "coding" are? We initially remain in some ways closed – consciously or un – to anything that makes us vulnerable and uncertain, because then, what would we do? The latter passages from **Madeline**'s abbreviated second letter below describe this phenomenon quite clearly and answer the question.

***

Gee's (2005) discourse analysis methods allow the researcher to construct a model based on seven building tasks. In my case, I was able to develop a preliminary discourse model of how learners of mathematics constructed learning by collaborating with each other (Gergen, 1999) and working with more knowledgeable others (Vygotsky, 1978).

Learners were working in an online public discussion forum called *The Math* Forum (located at http://www.mathforum.org). Dialogue took place in writing, through inter-textuality, organized as threads. Data transcripts were transformed into theorized transcripts, each including a story where participants tried to find support to develop different mathematical concepts.

This process turned out to be methodical; steps were followed in a similar way with all stories, until something started to jump out of the data. There was a voice calling out, looking for attention, making me go back to look for similar voices, as if together they had a special message to tell. In my blog I wrote the following entry: Wednesday, March 26, 2008

## VOICES CALLING OUT TO BE HEARD

Theorized transcriptions are ready and analysis for chapter six is on its way. Reading and re-reading the data made me take a moment to hear the voice of those searching for help. It was impressive, almost as if they were in agony trying to find a friendly hand that would pull them out of a hole. [It was the voice] … of those looking for help, of those who wanted to succeed in mathematics and could not find a way out by "themselves."

They were not only saying "I have this problem," it went deeper than that. …they were openly stating how confused they were… . And then, they "stopped," they "stop there" because they "don't understand."

I was not able to walk away from their cry. I felt I had to do something more with their search for meaning. There was nobody else. These were the learners that had no tutor, no individualized instruction, no helpful hand but that of being forum participants.

In the dissertation, I analyzed the help-seekers' identities among the forum participants. I also wrote a poem titled *"Voices calling out to be heard"* (pp. 156–157). It was not a choice, as I stated in the dissertation:

… [I] was called upon to hear what they were saying. Nothing mattered until [I] took time to hear their voices calling out for help. The cognitive analysis had to be suspended, as it was impossible to continue without paying attention to their cries. Help-seekers wanted to learn mathematics, but they needed the support from others. …. Once they were noticed, and once their cries were taken seriously, they set them aside and allowed the researcher to continue with the cognitive analysis of the chapter. (pp. 157–158)

This was something completely unexpected. Tension built up as the help-seekers cried for help and once they were heard, once they were taken seriously, they walked away.

I found out that data can speak to the researcher. By looking at data closely, by hearing the participants' voice, the researcher can act as a mediator that represents their interests.

***

My correspondents were not asking for help, they were offering it, yet I heard and 'felt' them much like Madeline describes. I realized they deserved to be heard, not merely "read." In coming to grips with the human courage, vulnerability, and tenacity demonstrated across their experiences, the powerful thinking and learning, I finally had to let into my own life the complexity of the task I was undertaking. I connected with it. I felt it; I felt them. I took a walk up my mountain (yes, 74 acres, 1700 feet above sea level, even a small, rushing waterfall in the spring), coming back to the work the next day, to the clumps of responses about the focus questions I had asked. In trying to figure out what they were "really" telling me, I began to ask "what *is* this letter you sent me? What is here that I am not reading?" Although I had already set aside 5 or 6 whole letters for inclusion "somewhere" to do "something", I realized that coding was getting in the way of the big picture, even as it had helped me get to know my correspondents and identify all that was "in there." How could I construct a genuine text without an overall conception about what was happening here, not from my codes (yes, they 'emerged' – or did I just find what I noticed?) but from their "wholes"? I decided I needed to figure out the questions each paragraph of each letter was answering, which became an exciting exercise. The idea of asking questions probably sounds simple to those who write about 'interrogating the text' or who guide middle schoolers through difficult writings. Yet, "discovering" this idea felt new and fresh because what I was learning – and not, led me to doing, which in turn led to understanding and renewed hope for the sense I was making.

My thinking and doing became congruent and explicit in action when I realized that in order to best understand what **Rosiare** was telling me, I had to "interview" her (see pp. 83–7); there were some gaps in what she was sharing with me. The question-answer format just "appeared" as I was note-asking. Although the interview format was neither planned nor a new template that worked across all letters, from it I learned to ask, again, what I was learning and how I was learning it. It is through this level of analysis I was able to understand what this book has to offer; data, codes, themes, questions all together helped illuminate the "big picture" that was there all along in the fluid thinking and reflecting of my correspondents related to our task.

Listening to my correspondents, then, has not only shaped your entrée into this book but also all that follows. Whether I knew it or not, I had internalized **Madeline**'s notion of "representing their interests"; the correspondents led my learning and shaped my decision making every step of the way, *once I got out of the way*! I started over yet again, with my re-marked-upon letters this time, but by now I began to see that portions I had "pruned away" in the second draft had a serious chance of being the correspondents' most meaningful reflecting, even if it was "too" long, a bit "wordy", or "not what I was looking for" at the time. Jeepers! How could I have done that? Their thinking lay in waiting for me, patiently. The correspondents themselves were and remain too kind to tell me I had "missed the point". I still may have in some cases, as not all of what was shared has found its way into this particular book. All errors in judgment are clearly mine.

From my new understanding, then, I began to compose abbreviated/ abridged letters for each correspondent, because I have only ever wanted this book to be an easy (read that as inexpensive!) book to own. In *this* letter, I used only their words but added a title of my "felt sense" of what was mattering to them to say. With this version of the correspondents' thinking/writing, I could be more linear and connected than the original letters sometimes were. As letter writers, we sometimes go back and forth in time and across ideas.

By mid-June, I sent this new material to them, seeking confirmation, edits, approval once again. I was thinking that maybe I had completed the last draft of our book? **Jessica**'s original letter, not much longer than what you will read below, is an example of the abbreviated format I used. In this case, I kept both the structure and responses **Jessica** used to address the questions she chose to write about.

1. *How did you learn about qualitative research?* As a master's student in education, I took a research design course that introduced me to multiple ways I could orient to the world and conduct research. With time, I began to realize that, for me, QR was indeed a lens that shaped and continually reshaped how I went about doing research, as well as how I made sense of the world. Drawing upon discourse theory and postcritical understandings of ethnography, I realize now that I was drawn to QR because of how I already orient to the world. As I engaged in my dissertation work, I came to realize that my political, social, and moral commitments are/were very much a part of the methodological choices I made, and always will be.

2. *Why did you choose it?* I was particularly drawn to methodologies that provided me with opportunity to explore complex and ambiguous phenomena. Further, I believe that QR can provide opportunity to offer cultural critiques and engage in discursive production that works to question taken-for-granted assumptions. Thus, my methodology of choice was very much related to what I hoped to do with the claims that I made. No longer did I desire to make abstract "hunches" without positioning them in relation to the data set. I hoped by engaging in qual work I would have the opportunity to shift my own understandings and proffer cultural critiques…

3. *What supports for it exist at your university?* I was gifted with multiple mentors. My dissertation committee included three qual methodologists who each functioned to support and challenge my data collection and analysis process. They enabled me to acquire Atlas.ti and Transana software training, attend multiple qual conferences and workshops across the U.S. and Europe, and participate in "writing and data sessions" in our university ethnographic and discourse analysis research team meetings. Without this support, I would indeed not have produced what I ultimately produced.

4. *What does the final form of your dissertation look like?* The final form of my dissertation was not considered to be traditional, as I constructed nine chapters versus our university's typical five. I began my dissertation with a poetic representation that took up and represented the popular discourses surrounding autism, and ended with a "response," constructed similarly with the words of my participants (as a response of sorts). I made these choices in relationship to my own commitments to my method, data, and the participants. I included an entire chapter on my positionality and another on the ways in which my theoretical understandings shifted as I engaged in the research process. My participants read each chapter, each interpretation,

with their responses being included in the final dissertation as well. This was particularly important to me as I aim to engage in relational approaches to research, attending always (I hope) to local knowledge and the participants from whom I have learned.

7. *Are there any stories you'd like to share from which others might learn?* The most important lesson was the way my relationship with the participants unfolded and ultimately shaped my interpretation of the data. When I first proposed my dissertation study, I had taken up the approach that many discourse analysts do: Proffer an interpretation, situate it in the data, and share it with a community of scholars. At my proposal defense, one of my mentors asked:

> What about face validity (Lather, 1986)? What about your participants' responses to your work? We've worked closely enough over the last years for me to know your commitments. I fear you will lose yourself if you do not return to the participants. Return to them. Ask them.

While I hesitated naming member checking as part of what I wanted to do, I simply responded with, "You are right—I must proceed in relation to my positionality and commitments as a researcher and community member. Thank you." In the end, I returned to the participants often, holding multiple gatherings and "data sessions" with them, all of which functioned to complicate my understanding and shape the ways in which I crafted my interpretations and implications. Through this experience, I have learned to assume that others see things I cannot see, as I remain limited by my own positionality. I approach my now completed dissertation work as still unfolding and always already partial, recognizing that relationality is central to everything that I name "research."

* * *

The book you are holding will probably disappoint a few of the correspondents who responded to my revised 'version' of their letter (abbreviated, reorganized, interview, etc.) with comments such as, "I loved my 'letter'"; it was "authentic"; it "met my intent perfectly". Some liked their titles, e.g., *"Expect the Unexpected"*, *"Live and Learn"*, *"A Quant goes Qual"*, *"Assert Yourself"*, *"My Favorite Method"*, *"The Opposite Sex"*, etc. Some did not respond at all. Regardless, it was the case that while they were reading and thinking, so was I. No one form of representation was helping me sort out and organize in any clear and useful way the multiple issues facing those who are using QR for their theses or dissertations, as you witnessed in Jessica's letter just above. So, in spite of getting strong encouragement for some of the draft pieces, I chose to compromise, again, deciding to use *all* of the aforementioned data analyses and representation strategies in order to bring forward what is valuable to be learned in a useful and useable way, a way that honors "prolonged engagement" and "saturation" with the data but does not dull the reader's reflective edge with the false familiarity a singular, standardized format tacitly allows.

Perhaps the *most* useful thing the various drafts were teaching me was how unimportant, in a sense, I was to all of this. Leaving me out of this writing was becoming easier and easier to do. I will never forget when I found myself identifying a correspondent, **Amy**, for example, and then continuing with her words as if she were "first" and not third person. I did not even catch what I was doing initially, because I was that tired. When I did notice, I got excited again. I wondered: Could I dare ask you, the reader, to make this cognitive "glide" as you read the material? That is, when you see a name in bold, think: 'Oh, **Amy** is telling me this; she is the "I" in this paragraph.' I tried it with a few more examples and then called a good friend and colleague, Judith Gouwens at Roosevelt University. I explained what was happening to me while writing. I asked her if I was crazy?! After listening, she replied it made sense to her on several levels.

With "permission to continue" received, I began removing my "**Amy** says:" and "**Bruce** writes" statements from some of the draft two portions still in use. Once again, the correspondents' writing appeared vibrant and "theirs" on the page. The pages began to read like a seminar class, where different individuals chimed in when they had something to add to the topic at hand. How could letters be like dialogue, a round table discussion? How could I get all of these folks "in the room" with the readers without me having to interrupt all of the time? This is the way, I thought, this is the way. Between deciding to go ahead with the "glide" and using some of the adapted letters, I felt I was finally, once again, well on the road to a final draft, which this book – one of many that could be – finally is.

# APPENDIX II

*The Process of Choosing Science, Technology, Engineering, and Mathematics Careers by Undergraduate Women: A Narrative Life History Analysis*

Roxanne M Hughes
*Florida State University*

# APPENDIX III



Given the emphasis on technology in the 21st century and **Wanju's** succinct email describing her work with young children and technology, I choose to share that email with you here.

I completed my dissertation, *Seeing the way they are in the way they IM: Case studies of Instant Messaging in Taiwanese fifth graders' lives*" in 2010. I had two major goals. First, I sought to understand the role of Yahoo! Messenger in a child's life. I asked three questions: (a) How is it related to the child's personal relationships? (b) How did it become a part of the child's Internet activities? and, (c) Where is it situated in the child's daily life? Second, I endeavored to obtain a larger picture of the child through observing the ways the child uses Yahoo! Messenger. In other words, I sought to understand how the child's IMing connected with his or her character, family values, and ideas about friendship. In order to achieve the goals of my research, I adopted the "participant as ally-essentialist portraiture approach" (Witz, 2006) research methodology, which argues that a researcher's task is not just to understand the investigated phenomenon but also to explore how the investigated phenomenon ties into the other aspects of the participant's life.

# REFERENCES


Alcott, L.M. (1868; 1872). *Little women.* Boston: Roberts Bros.

Allan, P.B. (1999, November). *The Sabbath bride: An example of art-based research.* Paper presented at the annual meeting of the American Art Association. Orlando, FL.

Appadurai, A. (1993). Patriotism and its futures. *Public Culture, 5*(3), 411–429.

———— (1999). Disjuncture and difference in the global cultural economy. In S. During (Ed.), *The cultural studies reader* (2nd ed.). pp. 220–230. New York: Routledge.

Au, W. (2008). Decolonizing the classroom: Lessons in multicultural education. *Rethinking Schools, 23*(2), 27–30.

Auerbach, C.F., & Silverstein, L.B. (2006). *Qualitative data: An introduction to coding and analysis.* New York: New York University Press.

Ball, S.J. (2006). *Education policy and the social class: the selected works of Stephen Ball.* New York: Taylor & Francis.

Barone, T. (1993). Ways of being at risk: The case of Billy Charles Barnett. In R. Donmoyer and R. Kos (Eds.), *At-risk students: Portraits, policies, programs, and practices.* (pp. 79–88). New York: SUNY Press.

Bhabha, H. (1985). Signs taken for wonders: Questions on ambivalence and authority under a tree outside Delhi, May 1817. *Critical Inquiry, 12*(1), 144–165.

Bogdan, R.C., & Biklen, S.K. (2003). *Qualitative research for education.* Boston: Allyn and Bacon.

Bolker, J. (1998). *Writing your dissertation in fifteen minutes a day: A guide to starting, revising, and finishing your doctoral thesis.* New York: Henry Holt and Company.

Bourdieu, P. (1977). *Outline of a theory of practice.* Cambridge: Cambridge University Press.

———— (1986). The forms of capital. In J. G. Richardson, (Ed.), *Handbook of theory and research for the sociology of education,* (pp. 241–58). New York: Greenwood.

———— (1996). *The state nobility: Elite schools in the field of power.* United Kingdom: Blackwell Publishing.

———— (2001). *Masculine domination.* California: Stanford University Press.

Brunner, C.C., Miller, M., & Hammel, K. (2003). Leadership preparation and the opposite of control: A technologically-delivered Deweyan approach. Annual meeting of the University Council of Educational Administration. Portland, Oregon.

Carroll, L. (1890s). *Alice in wonderland; and, Through the looking glass.* London: Collins.

Carter, P.L. (2003). "Black" cultural capital, status position, and schooling conflicts for low-income African American youth. *Social Problems, 50*(1), 136–155.

Cooperrider, D.L., Whitney, D., & Stavros. J.M. (2008). *Appreciative inquiry handbook: For leaders of change* (2nd ed.). San Francisco: Berret-Koehler Publishers.

Creswell, J. (1998; 2007). *Qualitative inquiry and research design: Choosing among five traditions.* Thousand Oaks, CA: Sage Publications.

———— (2005). *Educational research: planning, conducting, and evaluating quantitative and qualitative research* (2nd ed.). New Jersey: Prentice Hall.

Creswell, J., & Clark, V.L. Plano (2011). *Designing and conducting mixed methods research* (2nd ed.). Thousand Oaks, CA: Sage Publications.

Deaver, S., & McAuliffe, G. (2009). Reflective visual journaling during art therapy and counseling internships: A qualitative study. *Reflective Practice, 10*(5), 615–632.

Denzin, N.K., & Lincoln, Y.S. (2000). (Eds.). *Handbook of qualitative research* (2nd ed.). Thousand Oaks, CA: Sage Publications.

———— (2003). (Eds.). *Strategies of qualitative inquiry* (2nd ed.). Thousand Oaks, CA: Sage Publications.

———— (2005). *The SAGE handbook of qualitative research* (3rd ed.). Thousand Oaks, CA: Sage Publications.

Denzin, N.K., Lincoln, Y.S., & Giardina, M.D. (2006). Disciplining qualitative research. *International Journal of Qualitative Studies in Education, 19*(6), 769–782.

REFERENCES

Eisner, E. (1991). *The enlightened eye: Qualitative inquiry and the enhancement of educational practice.* NY, NY: Macmillan.

Fine, M., Weis, L., Weseen, S., & Wong, L. (2003). For whom? Qualitative research, representation, and social responsibilities. In N.K. Denzin and Y.S. Lincoln (Eds.), *The landscape of qualitative research: Theories and issues.* (2nd ed.). (pp. 166–207). Thousand Oaks, CA: Sage Publications.

Flanagan, J.C. (1954). *The critical incident technique.* Washington: American Psychological Association.

Friedman, J. (1992). Myth, history, and political identity. *Cultural Anthropology, 7*(2), 194–210.

Gee, J.P. (2005). *An introduction to discourse analysis: Theory and method.* NY: Routledge.

Gergen, K.J. (1999). *An invitation to social construction.* Thousand Oaks, CA: Sage Publications.

Glynos, J., Howarth, D., Norval, A., & Speed, E. (2009). *Discourse analysis: Varieties and methods.* U.K.: University of Essex.

Goodson, I., Biesta, G., Teddar, M., & Adair, N. (2010). *Narrative learning.* London: Routledge.

Hardt, M., & Negri, A. (2000). *Empire.* Cambridge, MA: Harvard University Press.

Ifedi, R.I. (2008). *African-born women faculty in the United States: Lives in contradiction.* Lewiston, NY: The Edwin Mellen Press.

Johnson, B.L., & Fauske, J.R. (2002). Principals and the political economy of environmental enactment. *Educational Administration Quarterly, 36*(2), 159–185.

Lather, P.A., & Smithies, C.S. (1997). *Troubling the angels: Women living with HIV/AIDS.* Boulder, CO: Westview Press.

Laura, C.T. (2010). Home/work: Engaging the methodological dilemmas and possibilities of intimate inquiry. *Race Ethnicity and Education, 13*(3), 227–293.

Levey, H. (2009). "Which one is yours?": Children and ethnography. *Qualitative Sociology, 32*(3), 311–331.

———— (2009). *Playing to win: Raising children in a competitive culture.* Princeton University Dissertation. *ProQuest.*

———— (2010). Trophies, triumphs, and tears: Children's experiences with competitive activities. *Sociological Studies of Children and Youth,* 319–349. Bingley, UK: Emerald Group Publishing.

Light, R.J., Singer, J.D., & Willett, J.B. (1990). *By design: Planning research on higher education.* Cambridge, MA: Harvard University Press.

Lightfoot, S.L. (1983). *The good high school.* NY: Basic Books.

Lyons, R. (1984). Autobiography: A reader for writers (2nd ed.). NY: Oxford University Press.

Marshall, C., & Rossman, G.B. (1999). *Designing qualitative research* (3rd ed.). Thousand Oaks, CA: Sage Publications.

Maxwell, J.A. (2005). *Qualitative research design: An interactive approach.* Thousand Oaks, CA: Sage Publications.

Meloy, J.M. (1994; 2002). *Writing the qualitative dissertation: Understanding by doing.* Mahwah, NJ: Lawrence Erlbaum Associates.

Merriam, S. (2009). *Qualitative research: A guide to design and implementation* (3rd ed.). San Francisco: Jossey-Bass.

Meyer, M.A. (2004). *Ho'oulu our time of becoming: Hawaiian epistemology, and early writings* (2nd ed.). Honolulu, HI: 'Ai Pohaku Press.

Mohanty, C.T. (1984). Under western eyes: Feminist scholarship through colonial discourse. *Boundary 2, 12*(3), 333–358.

Moustakas, C. (1994). *Phenomenological research methods.* Thousand Oaks, CA: Sage Publications.

Patton, M. (2002). *Qualitative research and evaluation methods* (3rd ed.). Thousand Oaks, CA: Sage Publications.

Piper, W. (1961; 1990). *The little engine that could.* NY: Platt & Munk.

Potter, W.J. (1996). *An analysis of thinking and research about qualitative methods.* Mahwah, NJ: Lawrence Erlbaum Associates.

Redmann, D.H., Lambrecht, J.J., & Stitt-Golden, W.L. (2000). The critical incident technique: A tool for qualitative research. *The Delta Pi Epsilon Journal, 42*(3), 132–153.

Seidman, I. (2006). *Interviewing as qualitative research: A guide for researchers in education and the social sciences* (3rd ed.). New York: Teachers College Press.

Van Manen, M. (1990). *Researching lived experience: Human science for an action sensitive pedagogy.* Albany, NY: SUNY Press.

Weed, M. (2005). "Meta-interpretation": A method for the interpretative synthesis of qualitative research. Forum: Qualitative Social Research, 6. Retrieved March 29, 2006 from http://www.qualitative-research.net/fqs/

———— (2008). A potential method for the interpretative synthesis of qualitative research: Issues in the development of meta-interpretation. *International Journal of Social Research Methodology, 11*(1), 13–28.

Wenger, E. (1998). *Communities of Practice: Learning, meaning and identity.* NY: Cambridge University Press.

Wilde, O. (1961). *Portrait tou Dorian Grey.* Delta.

Willis, P.E. (1997). *Learning to labor: How working class kids get working class jobs.* NY: Columbia University Press.

Witz, G. (2006). The participant as ally and essentialist portraiture. *Qualitative Inquiry, 12*(2), 246–268.

Yosso, T.J. (2005). Whose culture has capital? A critical race theory discussion of community cultural wealth. *Race, Ethnicity, and Education, 8*(1), 69–91.

# CORRESPONDENT INDEX

## ALPHABETICAL BY APPEARANCE ACROSS SECTIONS

*Correspondents Appearing in One Section N=17*

| Name/Intro | Section I | Section II | Section III | Section IV | Section V | Section VI + |
|---|---|---|---|---|---|---|
| Alex 12 | - | 92–4 | - | - | - | - |
| Annie 13 | - | 65–7 | - | - | - | - |
| Cassie 13 | - | - | - | 115, 118–20 | - | - |
| Chad 16 | - | 78–80 | - | - | - | - |
| Crystal 11 | 41–3 | - | - | - | - | - |
| Dennis v, 16 | - | - | - | - | - | - |
| Grover 12 | 25–6 | - | - | - | - | - |
| Hilary 15 | - | - | 103–5 | - | - | - |
| Jessica ix, 3, 14 | - | - | - | - | - | 149–50 |
| Jodi 14 | - | 97–9 | - | - | - | - |
| Kandace 12 | 48–50 | - | - | - | - | - |
| Karen H 16 | - | - | 101, 109–11 | - | - | - |
| Karen R 11 | - | 71–3 | - | - | - | - |
| Kristen 16 | - | - | - | - | 129–30 | - |
| Lisa H 8–10, 16 | - | - | - | - | - | - |
| Rosaire 14 | - | 83–7 | - | - | - | 148 |
| Sarah 11 | - | 67–70 | - | - | - | - |

*see also Madeline and Xyan next page

*Correspondents Appearing in Two Sections N=12*

| Name/Intro | Section I | Section II | Section III | Section IV | Section V | Section VI + |
|---|---|---|---|---|---|---|
| Aaron 14 | - | 57 | - | - | - | 136 |
| Brighid 16 | 32 | 60, 63, 96 | - | - | - | - |
| Carin 2, 11 | - | 75–6, 90 | 101, 107 | - | - | 137 |
| Debra 13 | 40 | 63, 74, 75 | - | - | - | - |

(*Continued*)

*Table (Continued)*

| Name/Intro | Section I | Section II | Section III | Section IV | Section V | Section VI + |
|---|---|---|---|---|---|---|
| Ellie 13 | 23, 47 | 90, 95 | - | - | - | - |
| Isabeau 15 | 26–7, 38, 51 | 91, 94 | - | - | - | - |
| Liz 11 | - | 58, 76 | - | - | - | 137–8 |
| Madeline* 14 | - | - | - | - | - | 146–7, 148 |
| Michelle 14 | - | 58, 65, 90, 95, 96 | 111 | - | - | - |
| Sharon 16 | 24 | 74, 75 | - | - | - | - |
| Sheila 4,13 | - | - | - | 122–4 | - | - |
| Xyan* 13 | - | - | - | 115–7 | - | - |

*Correspondents Appearing in 3 Sections N=17*

| Name/Intro | Section I | Section II | Section III | Section IV | Section V | Section VI + |
|---|---|---|---|---|---|---|
| Anabella 15 | 27, 40, 46 | 57, 82–3 | 108, 111 | - | - | - |
| Carita 16 | 38, 46 | 77 | - | 126 | - | - |
| Francesca 12 | 24, 38, 47 | 82, 95 | 106–7 | - | - | - |
| Isabelle viii, 14 | 23, 51 | 59, 76, 80 | 108, 111 | - | - | - |
| Jessie 13 | 26, 39 | - | 102, 109 | - | - | 142 |
| Joan 15 | 23, 46 | 73, 94 | 105 | - | - | - |
| Julie 12 | 23, 38 | 56 | 112 | - | - | - |
| Katherine 15 | 23–4, 38, 47–8, 50 | - | 109 | 118, 124 | - | - |
| Keith 15 | - | 76–7 | - | - | 131–2 | 137 |
| Lisa W 12 | 47 | 87, 92 | 105 | - | - | - |
| Megan 14 | 27, 39 | 61–2 | - | - | - | 136 |
| Michele 15 | 30 | 56, 58, 81 | - | - | - | 138, 139–141, 146 |
| Monica Jean 14 | 27 | 74 | - | - | - | 143 |
| Rich 12 | 17–18, 29–30, 35, 45, 52 | 56 | - | - | - | 135, 142 |
| Roxanne 11 | 28–9, 30, 46 | 65, 74, 80, 95 | - | - | - | 153–4 |
| Tom 11 | 23 | 60–1, 64, 96 | 102–3, 108 | - | - | - |
| Veronica 11 | - | 64, 81 | 103 | 120, 125 | - | - |

### Correspondents Appearing in 4 Sections N=17

| Name/Intro | Section I | Section II | Section III | Section IV | Section V | Section VI + |
|---|---|---|---|---|---|---|
| Amanda 14 | 26, 39, 46 | 56 | 109, 111 | - | - | 141 |
| Amy 12 | 28, 37, 51 | 62–3, 91 | - | 126 | - | - |
| Angela F 12 | 51 | 60, 67, 73, 95 | 105, 106, 108–09 | - | - | 135, 141–2 |
| Angela LV 15 | 27–8, 40–1, 51 | 77, 89-90 | 113–14 | - | 132–4 | - |
| Anonymous Excerpt 14 | 40 | 59, 102, 103 | 105, 106, 107, 109 | 125, 126 | - | - |
| Bruce 16 | 29, 38 | 94 | 105 | - | - | - |
| Cassandra vii, 15 | 24–5 | 55, 80–1, 91 | 111–12 | 121 | - | - |
| Cindy 12 | 39–40, 50 | 53, 60, 65, 74–5, 80 | 103, 112 | - | 134 | - |
| Donna 12 | 29, 47 | 74, 81–2 | 102, 109 | 125 | - | - |
| Ginny 11 | 27 | 57 | 106 | - | 130–1 | - |
| Jim B 2, 7, 16 | 17, 21, 24, 32, 38, 46 | 58, 67, 95 | 111 | 121–2 | - | - |
| Jim O 11 | 23, 37, 46 | 63–4, 76, 90, 96–97 | 105 | - | - | 141 |
| Kj 13 | 38, 51 | 57, 90, 91–2 | - | 128 | - | 142 |
| Monica 16 | - | 62, 90, 95 | 101, 105 | 115 | - | 141 |
| Nancy 11 | 31–2, 47 | 57, 97 | - | 127 | 130 | - |
| Shaunna 14 | 22–3, 36–7 | - | - | 117, 120–1, 128 | - | 138–9 |
| Tiffany 15 | 40, 51 | 55, 96 | 111 | - | - | 136 |

### Correspondents Appearing in 5 and 6 sections N=7

| Name/Intro | Section I | Section II | Section III | Section IV | Section V | Section VI + |
|---|---|---|---|---|---|---|
| Corey 13 | 23 | 56 | 106 | 126–7 | 130 | 143 |
| Kristan 15 | 30, 38 | 65 | 106, 107 | - | 132 | 136 |
| Mary 7, 16 | 23, 33, 39, 46 | 73, 87, 94-5, 96 | 106, 107, 112 | 126 | - | 136 |
| Ronn 11 | 38–9, 50–1 | 62 | 107 | 124–25, 126 | - | 138 |
| Sandy 7, 12 | 27, 46 | 65 | 106, 108 | 126 | 129, 130 | - |
| Vic vii, 13 | 30, 38 | 60, 95 | 102, 111 | - | 130 | 141 |
| Wanju vii, 16 | 23 | 73 | - | 121 | 134 | 145, 155 |

# CORRESPONDENT LIST

Debra Ackerman (2006) Ph.D.
Monica Jean Alaniz (2010) Ph.D.
Jessie Guidry Baginski (2011) Ph.D.
Carin Barber (2010) Ed.D.
James P. Barber (2009) Ph.D.
Sandra Blanchette (2010) Ed.D.
Kristen Chorba, graduate student
Aaron Coe (2011) Ed.D.
Thomas Conway (2010) Ph.D.
Amanda Corbin-Staton (2009) Ed.D.
Virginia (Ginny) Cottrill, graduate
    student
Cassandra Crute (2010) Ph.D.
Sarah Deaver (2009) Ph.D.
Isabelle Drewelow (2009) Ph.D.
Francesca Durand (2011) Ph.D.
Brighid Dwyer (2012)
Cynthia Epperson (2010) Ph.D.
Elizabeth Farley-Ripple (2008) Ph.D.
Victor Fisher (2010) Ed.D.
Jodi Fisler (2011) Ph.D.
Shelia Fram (2008) Ph.D.
Angela Frusciante (2004) Ph.D.
Nancy Gray (2009) Ph.D.
Richard Grogan (2010) Ph.D.
Ronald Hallett (2009) Ph.D.
Karen Hammel (2008) Ed.D.
Carita Harrell (2008) Ed.D.
Lisa Heuvel (2011) Ed.D.
Keith Higa (2010) Ph.D.
Wanju Huang (2010) Ph.D.
Roxanne Hughes (2010) Ph.D.
Rosaire Ifedi (2007) Ed.D.
Bruce Ingraham, graduate student
Isabeau Iqbal, graduate student
Annie Jonas (2011) Ed.D.

Kandace Knudson (2005) Ph.D.
Crystal Laura (2011) Ph.D.
Tiffany Leger-Rodriguez (2010) Ph.D.
Jessica Lester (2011) Ph.D.
Hilary Levey Friedman (2009) Ph.D.
Julie Levine (2011) Ed.D.
Angela Lopez-Velasquez (2008) Ph.D.
Katherine Cumings Mansfield (2011)
    Ph.D.
Anabella Martinez (2009) Ed.D.
Michelle McConkey (2012) DMA
Dennis McCunney, graduate student
Grover McDaniel (2009) Ph.D.
Corey McKenna (2007) Ph.D.
Alex Medler (2008) Ph.D.
Joan Q. Minnis (2011) Ed.D.
Monica Morita, graduate student
Xyanthe Neider (2010) Ph.D.
Megan Ohler (2009) Ed.D.
James Olive (2009) Ph.D.
Amy Orange, graduate student
Madeline Ortiz-Rodriguez (2008) Ph.D.
Shaunna Payne Gold (2010) Ed.D.
Michele Paynter Paise (2010) DMA
Cassie Quigley (2010) Ph.D.
Veronica Richard (2010) Ph.D.
Kelley-Jean Strong-Rhoads (2011) Ed.D.
Yeon Sun (Ellie) Ro (2010) Ph.D.
Karen Ross, graduate student
Donna Sayman (2009) Ph.D.
Chad Timm (2008) Ph.D.
Kristan Venegas (2005) Ph.D.
Lisa Weaver (2006) Ph.D.
Sharon Woodlief (2010) Ph.D.
Mary E. Zamon (2009) Ph.D.

# SUBJECT INDEX

*Necessarily Imperfect & Incomplete: Build your Own!*